A Parent's Guide to
Band and
Orchestra

Jim Probasco

BETTERWAY PUBLICATIONS, INC.
WHITE HALL, VIRGINIA

Published by Betterway Publications, Inc.
P.O. Box 219
Crozet, VA 22932
(804) 823-5661

Cover photographs by Tim Sams and Gabriel Kuperminc
Text photographs by Jim Probasco
Funky Winkerbean strips reprinted with special permission of
    North American Syndicate, Inc.
Typography by Park Lane Associates

Library of Congress Cataloging-in-Publication Data

Probasco, Jim
        A parent's guide to band and orchestra / Jim Probasco.
            p. cm.
        Includes bibliographical references and index.
        ISBN 1-55870-183-4 : $7.95
            1. Music--Instruction and study--Juvenile. 2. Musical
instruments--Instruction and study. 3. Bands (Music)--Instruction
and study. 4. Orchestra--Instruction and study. I. Title.
        MT740.P68 1991
        784.0240431--dc20   90-20951
                                                                          CIP
                                                                          MN

Printed in the United States of America
0 9 8 7 6 5 4 3 2 1

[handwritten notes:]
1. music - Study and teaching.
2. musical instruments - study and teaching.
3. Bands (music) - Study and teaching.
4. Orchestra - study and Teaching.
E

To Jan, Dana, Brad, and Erika
for their patience and encouragement.

And to Mom P.
for asking if I wanted to learn how to play an instrument.

ACKNOWLEDGMENTS

If I tried to acknowledge all the parents, students, fellow teachers, and school administrators I've known over the past seventeen years who contributed to the writing of this book, it would take a forklift to move it!

So, instead, I'll thank a few special folks and probably have a whole bunch more mad at me. Which, come to think of it, isn't much different from the Spring Band Banquet!

Harry Dinkle's "dad," Tom Batiuk, urged me to write this book when I first told him of my idea several years ago. From time to time, Tom called and asked how the project was coming along. Thanks, in part, to Tom's encouragement (or harassment, depending on the time of the phone call) I finally got it done.

I am grateful to Clair Miller, Music Coordinator for the Kettering City Schools, for teaching me a few things about teaching, especially about the "Exploratory Period" — the best way I know to start your child on an instrument.

Jerry Hauer and the employees of Hauer Music provided helpful information from the music dealer's perspective. And Bob Sherman, manager of the Baroque Violin Shop, and his staff filled in a lot of blank spaces for me regarding renting, selling, and maintaining stringed instruments.

Most of the photographs in this book were processed by Bill Aldrich at "Pan-a-View." Bill spent many hours making my "snapshots" look more professional than they should have.

Pat Hiatt, Past President of the National Association of Professional Band Instrument Repair Technicians, provided valuable information about maintenance and repair of instruments. (Pat also showed me how to net a walleye with one hand while opening a pull top with the other. But that's another story!)

Thanks to Bob Hostage, Editor-in-Chief at Betterway Publications, for allowing this book to happen, and to Hilary Swinson and Tim Sams for making it happen.

Finally, I want to thank my family, especially my wife, Jan, for letting me write all summer and only once asking me to "mow the siding" or "paint the lawn" or whatever it was she said.

The book is done, just as another school year begins. My face is unshaven, bright light makes me squint, and I smell like roadkill. But it's time to nuke a bowl of cheese popcorn, kids. Dad's coming up from the basement!

FOREWORD

When I was in elementary school, I joined the band . . . or the band joined me, I'm still not sure which. I did it with all the forethought and preparation that I usually gave to going out to recess. I then marched home and proudly announced my decision to my parents who were, no doubt, somewhat dumbfounded by this sudden turn of events.

Little consideration was given to consideration of an instrument (I picked the trombone . . . or it picked me, I'm still not sure which), or whether to buy an instrument or use one owned by the school (looking back on it, the school's horn really shouldn't have been touched without a tetanus booster shot). Or to the fact that I'd soon be wearing braces, or would soon be needing a ride home from school after practice, etc., etc.

All of this led to numerous trials and tribulations that somehow my family and I managed to muddle through. In the end, everything turned out okay, so that these days, as I chronicle the adventures of Harry L. Dinkle, the world's greatest band director, I can look back and laugh at some of the trying times my family and I encountered. If we had Jim's book back then, we could have avoided most of the trials and tribulations. However, I would have had a lot less to write about, and my cartoon career might never have gotten off the ground.

So I want to thank Jim for waiting until now to write this book that you hold in your hands. By allowing me to do it the hard way, he saved my career, and by making it easier for the next generation of band students, he'll keep any budding cartoonists from getting too much good material.

Tom Batiuk

CONTENTS

Running for Office
Working with the Band or Orchestra Teacher
How to Complain
Recap

The "No Guarantee" Guarantee
"Take the Other Stick"

A. Instrument Price Comparison Sheet
B. Monthly Record of Home Practice
C. Selected Instrument Manufacturers
D. Other Mail Order Sources
E. Selected Associations, Magazines, Insurance

INTRODUCTION

It's three o'clock. The front door swings open. A multi-colored blur races down the hall past the living room and jettisons a twenty-seven pound book bag which slams to the floor, landing inches from the dog. The dog yelps, jumps over the sofa, and crashes into the wall.

For most parents, it's a typical school day afternoon. This time, however, there's a twist. The blur reaches the kitchen, jerks open the refrigerator door, lifts a milk jug to its lips and yells, "GUESS WHAT? I WANT TO PLAY AN INSTRUMENT!"

If you are like most parents, this declaration will generate feelings of joy and panic. Joy because your child wants to participate in something educational, wholesome, and fun; panic because you haven't the faintest idea what to do next!

That's what this book is all about: *what to do next*. This book is designed to help take the mystery out of your child's band or orchestra experience and show you how to foster those first tentative steps in this fascinating new adventure.

For children to be successful in anything — academics, sports, music — parents must be actively involved in the learning process. In other words, they must provide support. Unfortunately, as schools employ greater numbers of educational "experts," parents have begun to feel that they simply don't have the knowledge or skills to help their child — particularly when it comes to specialized activities such as band or orchestra.

The truth is, your involvement can mean the difference between success and failure when it comes to your child's music education. You don't need a degree in music. You don't need to know how to play an instrument. You don't even need to know how to read music. All you need is a sincere desire to support your child as he begins this exciting journey.

In this book, I've tried to answer questions most often asked by parents during my seventeen years as a public school music teacher. Questions such as:

How can I tell whether my child can learn to play a band or orchestra instrument? (Chapter 1)

How do we choose an instrument? (Chapter 2)

How much does it cost? (Chapter 3)

What instrument would you recommend for a child who can break rocks with his teeth? (A Nerf® drum set)

You can read the book from cover to cover for an overview of the entire process of joining band or orchestra, then use it as a reference to look up information when specific questions arise.

Each chapter explores a different facet of your child's band or orchestra experience and concludes with a brief review of the chapter's main points. Several helpful appendices provide everything from instrument price comparison forms to names and addresses of instrument manufacturers, mail order music dealers, music-related gifts, associations, magazines, and much more.

This book will, I hope, help you and your child better understand the process of joining band or orchestra; choosing, buying, and maintaining an instrument; and building the skills necessary for your child to grow as a musician.

It will also help you, as a parent, understand the importance of your involvement in your child's music education.

Learning to play a musical instrument is not easy. Your child will spend a lot of time and effort developing the skills and discipline required to work as a member of a "music team." You and your child will learn to deal with the frustration that accompanies this new learning process.

Your patience and love (not to mention pain threshold) will be tested many times as you listen to your child practice his instrument — each "thump," "blatt," and "squeak" giving new meaning to the term "noise pollution."

Perseverance, devotion (and a good pair of industrial strength earplugs) will see you through, however, and you will get your reward. It will come one magic evening when you sit in the auditorium, watching and listening as your child — the one who peeled paint from the bedroom walls with sounds even Stephen King couldn't dream up — plays those first few notes in public performance.

It is a moment a parent treasures forever; one, I hope, you and your child share soon.

As a bonus, when your child joins band or orchestra, you gain admission to a unique organization. You become a member of one of the most enthusiastic, involved, fun loving, supportive, just-plain-crazy groups of people around.

You become a "Music Parent."

So, what are we waiting for? Let's get started!

1.

GETTING STARTED

Like many parents, you may think the ability to play a musical instrument is a "gift." You may believe that children who are born with this "gift" can learn to play an instrument — those without the gift can only listen. This, simply, is not true.

YOUR CHILD CAN PLAY AN INSTRUMENT

Your child does not have to be able to play trumpet like Doc Severinsen or violin like Itzhak Perlman to be a member of the school band or orchestra. Almost four million young people play band and orchestra instruments in this country. Very few of them are "gifted" musicians, yet most are happy, contributing participants in their school music programs.

Learning to play an instrument is, chiefly, a matter of developing a set of skills. These are skills any child can learn — like tying shoes or playing video games.

And, as with all important life skills — such as tying shoes (and playing video games) — some children learn faster than others. Given enough time and sufficient interest, however, any child can learn them. If you don't believe me, ask yourself this: Do you know any child who can't play video games? Of course not. Children aren't born knowing how to play Super Mario Brothers® yet, somehow, they all learn.

The physical coordination and mental skills required for a child

Your child can learn to play an instrument.

to learn to play a musical instrument are no more complex than those required to play many video games. The problem is, so much emphasis has been placed on "creative genius" that we have all become brainwashed into believing that only those children who possess some sort of "magic" can do it.

In the real world, "magic" is also a skill. The foundation of magic is little more than a set of well-rehearsed skills or tricks. And so it is with learning to play an instrument. Ninety percent of learning to play a band or orchestra instrument involves developing physical and mental skills.

In a nutshell, your child can learn to play an instrument. All it takes is interest.

Some children need encouragement. Some children hesitate to bring up playing a musical instrument because they are afraid of failure or perhaps because the idea just hasn't occurred to them.

That was the case with me when I was in seventh grade. My mother asked, one day, whether I would like to learn to play an instrument. If she hadn't asked, I might never have started playing the trombone. The notion of joining band just hadn't occurred to me.

Even if the subject hasn't come up, ask your child whether he has thought about joining band or orchestra. You might be pleas-

Joining band or orchestra saves wear and tear on your stainless steel cookware!

antly surprised at the answer you get.

The recipe for your child's success as a band or orchestra musician, then, contains two key ingredients: (1) Interest — Your child must *want* to learn to play an instrument; and (2) Support — *You* must take an active interest in your child's musical experience.

MUSIC IS BASIC

Music enhances the quality of our lives, and it surrounds us every day. Can you remember ever going through a day without hearing at least some kind of music? Probably not. Music is so much a part of our culture that to imagine life without it is almost impossible. In short, music is an essential part of daily life.

As important as music is then, the role it plays in your child's life should include more than listening to records, watching MTV, and attending concerts. Music is not passive, it is active. Music is something we *do*.

Most children love to perform—either by singing or playing an instrument. Remember when, as a toddler, your child danced and sang in front of the TV or made a drum set out of a wastebasket

Playing an instrument is an investment that lasts a lifetime.

Youngsters join band or orchestra to have fun and be with friends.

and your stainless steel cookware? Joining band or orchestra offers your child an excellent opportunity to perform or *do* music (and it saves a lot of wear and tear on that stainless steel cookware). Helping to fulfill your child's basic need to make music is only one of the many benefits membership in band or orchestra provides.

In addition to developing a whole new set of physical and mental skills, your child will also learn: responsibility, self-discipline, a feeling of self-worth, and the value of cooperation.

While it's true that your child can learn most of these values in other activities, such as playing football or cheerleading, playing an instrument will enhance your child's life for many years to come, long after football and cheerleading are nothing more than a few faded pictures in the school yearbook. In other words, you can do music a lot longer than you can do many other activities.

During part of the winter, I direct a community concert band with more than one hundred members ranging in age from eighteen to eighty. This active group performs many concerts annually and has toured Europe and Canada several times.

Members of this musical organization started like your child, as youngsters who wanted to learn to play an instrument. Some of them are excellent musicians, some are average, but all have richer, fuller lives because they made a decision to *do* music.

Learning to play an instrument involves your child in an activity that helps build important social skills and reinforces a positive sense of self-worth. Most important, playing an instrument meets a basic need to make music and exposes your child to an understanding of the fine arts in a way not possible through listening alone. Not only that, but it's an investment that lasts a lifetime. What better reasons could there be for joining?

BAND AND ORCHESTRA ARE FUN

Now that we have established the reasons children *should* join band or orchestra, let's examine the reasons they *do*.

Remember our video game example earlier? It's probably safe to say that playing video games is a skill most children would gladly spend their entire adolescent life learning. They don't do this because they want to make the world a better place. They do it because they and their friends think it's neat to throw exploding vegetables at characters on a TV screen! In other words, it's fun and "everybody else is doing it."

Most children join band or orchestra for the same reasons: (1) playing an instrument sounds like fun; and (2) all their friends are joining.

Youngsters *join* band or orchestra for reasons much different from the ones that keep them in. There is nothing wrong with this, we just need to recognize it.

Remember: We are talking about your child joining an instrumental music performing group, not a street gang. I doubt that you will ever have to go downtown to bail your "Marching Artichoke" or "Fiddling Firefly" out of the slammer for harassing subway riders with off-key renditions of "Stars and Stripes Forever."

The point is this: Children are not motivated to join band or orchestra by a deep love for music. With your encouragement, and the guidance of a knowledgeable, caring, teacher, the love will come in its own good time.

WHEN DOES THE FUN BEGIN?

Most beginning band and orchestra programs start in the fifth or sixth grade (age ten or eleven). Some schools start youngsters as early as the fourth grade, but this practice is fading, primarily because the dropout rate for very young children is astronomical. Most fourth graders are not physically ready to play full-size instruments.

In most schools, a letter announcing beginning band and orchestra classes is sent home at the beginning of the school year in which your child is eligible to join. The letter usually tells how to sign your child up for band or orchestra; whether any aptitude or readiness tests are given; and when the classes actually begin.

If your child's school starts beginners in fifth grade and your youngster is in sixth, you might assume your child has missed out by not joining at the earlier age.

That's probably not true. Not all children are ready to start on a musical instrument at the same age, so most schools allow for more than one entry point into the band and orchestra program.

Many schools even have beginning programs in middle school or junior high.

If your child has missed the start of the regular school program and still wants to join, you might consider paying for private lessons to allow your child to catch up. Most music teachers can recommend a good private teacher and will be happy to evaluate your child's progress after a few weeks of study to determine whether the child is ready to join the regular band or orchestra program.

SUZUKI STRING METHOD

One exception to not starting children on a band or orchestra instrument before the fifth or sixth grade is the Suzuki String Program, also known as the Suzuki Talent Education Program. Developed by Shinichi Suzuki, a Japanese music teacher, the Talent Education Program supports a whole network of private music classes in which children as young as preschool age are taught to play "down size" (miniature) stringed instruments.

In the Suzuki system, children are taught to play by rote (repetition and imitation) with guidance from a teacher and lots of involvement by the parents. The theory behind the Suzuki approach is that since all children learn their native tongue by imitation and repetition, they can also learn to play a musical instrument the same way.

As an educational theory it sounds like a good idea. But educational theories are plentiful and only cost about two dollars a pound at your local bookstore. What matters is what works.

String teachers have widely varying opinions of the Suzuki system. Many consider it the backbone of the school orchestra program and would be happy if all their students started on Suzuki instruments. Others disagree with Suzuki's emphasis on rote learning and feel that it's difficult to teach Suzuki students to read music when they have spent so much time learning to play by ear. Most school string programs, however, incorporate both Suzuki and non-Suzuki students into the orchestra with few problems.

If your child's school has an orchestra, chances are there are Suzuki classes somewhere near you. Suzuki classes are not normally a part of the regular school music program, but if there are Suzuki classes in your area, the school string teacher will know about them.

If you want more information about the Suzuki Talent Education Program, you can ask your school's orchestra teacher or write the Suzuki Association of the Americas, listed in Appendix E.

MUSIC APTITUDE TESTS

Some schools screen potential band and orchestra members by administering music aptitude tests. Tests of musical aptitude are designed to measure "musical talent" or "I.Q." Measures of musical talent, as you might imagine, are about as controversial as regular I.Q. tests.

First of all, we're not even sure what "musical talent" is. Is a child "talented," for example, if he can listen to music with pleasure and understanding? Or is talent only reflected in those who sing or play instruments?

There are many questions and few good answers. Despite the controversy, respected aptitude tests, such as the Gordon Music Aptitude Profile, can help determine musical strengths and weaknesses and can be used to guide your child's learning should he decide to join the school band or orchestra. Music aptitude tests can also help teachers identify talented children who should be encouraged to participate in the band or orchestra program.

Unfortunately, even the best aptitude tests can be misused. Sometimes the results of music aptitude tests are used to discourage or even prevent a child from participating in band or orchestra. No music aptitude test should ever be used to keep an interested child out of band or orchestra. Music aptitude tests can only reveal musical strengths and weaknesses. No test has been devised that can determine whether or not your child will be successful as an instrumental musician.

TESTS OF ADAPTATION

Some tests or surveys evaluate your child by discussing such things as length of arms, independence of hands, thickness of lips, and various other physical attributes.

Physical characteristics play no role in determining your child's musical aptitude. Physical characteristics can, however, play a role in choosing an instrument, once the decision to join has been made. (Chapter 2 has more information on the role of physical characteristics in the selection of an instrument.) One note of caution: If your child has serious physical limitations, the choice of instruments may be limited. Your school's orchestra or band teacher can help if this is the case with your child.

If your child's school administers aptitude tests or tests of adaptation as part of the process of joining band or orchestra, the results should be explained to you. Knowing the nature of your child's musical strengths and weaknesses will help you understand the teacher's evaluation of your child's progress later on.

TALKING WITH THE GENERAL MUSIC TEACHER

The general music teacher — the teacher your child has for music class — can provide some information about your child's readiness and interest in learning to play a musical instrument. General music classes often include pre-band/orchestra instruments, such as Flutophone® or recorder. This usually happens in third or fourth grade, before regular instruction in band or orchestra begins. Ask your child's general music teacher whether the school provides such instruction and if so, how your child did.

OTHER CONSIDERATIONS

In most middle schools, children have separate, scheduled band and orchestra classes. Therefore, if your child joins band or orchestra, he will not be taken out of another academic class to participate.

In the elementary grades, however, your child will probably miss some regular class time to participate in instrumental music. Talk with your child's elementary classroom teacher to find out how much regular class time the child will miss, and how missed work is to be made up.

*General music classes often include instruction on pre-band/
orchestra instruments such Flutophone® or recorder.*

Many elementary classroom teachers plan review or quiet study for the rest of the class when children are out for special activities such as band or orchestra. But, as the number of these special classes increases, classroom teachers are finding it more difficult to get through their lesson plans in the time left.

Knowing you care about your child's classroom progress will make a difference to your child's classroom teacher and might influence the teacher's plans when your child is out of the room.

If your child falls behind in class or fails to stay caught up with homework, the classroom teacher might suggest he drop out of band or orchestra. Before you take such a drastic step, discuss the problem with your child, the classroom teacher, and the band or orchestra teacher.

Band or orchestra can be a powerful motivating force for a child who loves to play an instrument. It might make the difference for a child who is teetering between success and failure in class. In any event, it just makes sense to discuss alternatives before you take action.

Since playing an instrument involves learning new skills, time must be set aside for practice at home. It doesn't take much — only ten to fifteen minutes a day at first — but your child will not progress without it. Your child should not have so many outside of school activities that there is no time to practice. If your child's schedule is too full, you might have to make some hard decisions about which activities to keep and which to drop.

Finally, cost certainly figures into the decision to join band or orchestra. It's not hard to end up spending several hundred dollars on an instrument once the initial rental period is over. If you add in the cost of books and optional private lessons, membership in band or orchestra can be very expensive indeed.

Ways exist to reduce or spread out the cost of participation. For example, your child might be able to obtain a school-owned instrument for a very low annual rental fee, thereby eliminating the biggest expense — buying an instrument. (See Chapter 3 for more information.)

RECAP

- Your child can learn to play a band or orchestra instrument if he wants to.
- Playing an instrument helps fulfill your child's basic need to perform music.
- Don't worry if your child wants to join band or orchestra for "non-musical" reasons. That's normal.
- Band and orchestra usually begins in fifth or sixth grade.
- Your child can start on a stringed instrument as early as preschool age through Suzuki classes.
- Results of music aptitude tests should be used to guide learning.
- The general music teacher can tell you how your child performed on pre-band/orchestra instruments.
- Your child's classroom teacher can tell you how missed class time is to be made up.
- If your child gets behind in class, don't decide to drop band or orchestra before discussing alternatives with teachers.
- Review your child's schedule. You may need to eliminate some activities to make room for band or orchestra.
- There are ways to reduce the cost of participating in band or orchestra so it will fit into your budget.

Reprinted with special permission of North America Syndicate, Inc.

See how easy getting started is? There's really no mystery to it at all. For your child, it's a matter of making a decision to perform music. For you, it's a matter of providing encouragement and support. Next step: Choosing an instrument.

2.

CHOOSING AN INSTRUMENT

Once your child decides to play an instrument, the next step is choosing one. The instrument your child chooses will determine whether he will join band or orchestra.

BAND OR ORCHESTRA — WHAT'S THE DIFFERENCE?

"Beginning Orchestra" refers to the stringed instruments—violin, viola, cello, and bass. Later, in junior high and high school, players from the band are added and the group is called "Full" Orchestra.

Following this logic, you might assume that an orchestra without band musicians would be called "Empty" Orchestra. It's not — it's called "String" Orchestra.

"Beginning Band" includes the wind instruments (flute, clarinet, saxophone, trumpet, and trombone) and percussion (snare drum and bells).

Orchestra has been around much longer, but band is more popular by a wide margin. Today, only one out of every ten school districts has an orchestra program. This is due, in part, to two elements of the high school band program that orchestra doesn't offer — marching band and jazz band.

The marching band is the colorful, entertaining, uniformed group that performs during halftime at football games and participates in marching band contests and festivals.

Beginning orchestra refers to the stringed instruments . . .

. . . and band includes winds and percussion.

The jazz ensemble, actually an outgrowth of the dance band, consists of saxophones, trumpets, trombones, and a rhythm section (piano, guitar, bass, and drums). Jazz ensembles also enter contests and festivals and even perform at basketball games in many schools.

In order to make string programs more attractive, many school orchestras have added a group called "strolling strings." The idea for strolling strings comes from a musical group at the White House — the Air Force Strolling Strings. Strolling strings function sort of like a walking jazz band.

Strolling strings perform at banquets, receptions, and other activities, while "strolling" from table to table. Not all orchestra programs have them, but strolling strings are rapidly gaining in popularity in schools across the country.

Though your child's choice of an instrument determines which of the two groups (band or orchestra) he will join, it's important to compare your child's interests and personality with the kinds of musical activities he will encounter as a member of either group.

Differences between band and orchestra are greater in high school than they are in the elementary grades. Chapter 8 provides more information about those differences, and you may want to review them before your child makes a choice.

INSTRUMENTS THAT APPEAL TO YOUR CHILD

Children often have a particular instrument in mind when they decide they want to join band or orchestra. I don't recommend encouraging your child to play the instrument he thinks he wants to play, especially if this is before he has had a chance to try different instruments.

Choosing the right instrument is critical to your child's success in band or orchestra. When your child comes home from school and tells you he wants to join band or orchestra, your first question will probably be: "What instrument do you want to play?"

The problem is, your child has no real basis for choosing an instrument. A child's first choice of an instrument is often a product of the same logic that got him interested in joining band or orchestra in the first place. That is, he wants to play whichever instrument his friends want to play, or the instrument that seems like it will be the most fun.

Popular choices for instruments seem to vary with the tide and phases of the moon. Two of today's most popular choices are saxophone and drums, primarily due to the proliferation of rock videos. All the glitz and glamor of MTV will be precious little consolation to you or your child, however, if he finds out he can't play the saxophone or doesn't like the drums as much as he thought he would. This can be especially troubling to parents who just took out a third mortgage on the house to pay for an expensive drum set that ends up being used as a card table or clothes hamper in their child's room.

GETTING HELP FROM THE BAND OR ORCHESTRA TEACHER

Getting advice from the music teacher before choosing an instrument might seem like the obvious thing to do, but there are plenty of parents who go to a music store before their child joins band or orchestra and, with absolutely no idea what they are doing, buy or rent an instrument for the following school year.

Rule Number One when it comes to choosing an instrument for your child is: *Don't do anything without discussing it with the band or orchestra teacher.*

THE RECRUITING PROGRAM

Most schools have an established program for recruiting students into band and orchestra. When your child comes home and says he wants to play an instrument, it is probably the result of that recruiting program.

A typical band and orchestra recruiting program might start with the administration of some form of music aptitude test to all eligible students. As discussed in Chapter 1, the results of these tests can be used to guide learning for all children who enroll in the instrumental program, or to encourage children with potential who don't show initial interest.

After aptitude testing is completed, the teacher will probably demonstrate instruments in the classroom, explain the instrumental music program, and answer questions.

A meeting for parents and interested children will then be held at school to explain the instrumental program; or letters outlining the program will be sent home, encouraging interested students to sign up for band or orchestra.

An individual conference with parents and student may follow, in which aptitude test results and the child's interests are discussed. Sometimes these conferences include a discussion of physical characteristics and even some "hands on" playing of different instruments before selection is made. Some schools have a long-term hands-on program, called an "Exploratory Period," in which children get to try various instruments before making a choice.

In a few schools, instrument assignment is made at an evening parent meeting when a music dealer explains the instrument rental program, squints at the child and says: "You look like a clarinet player, kid. Here, take this." Obviously, the "squint" system of instrument assignment is less than ideal. The best way for your child to choose an instrument is through some form of exploratory period.

TRYING DIFFERENT INSTRUMENTS — THE EXPLORATORY PERIOD

Schools that have adopted an exploratory period as part of beginning band and orchestra encourage children to try several instruments over a period of time — anywhere from one to several weeks — until they find one that they like to play and do well with.

During the exploratory period in the school system where I teach, we use the four main stringed instruments — violin, viola, cello, and bass — and the band instruments beginners usually start on — flute, clarinet, cornet (trumpet), trombone, and percussion.

I have one each of the various instruments and, during the exploratory period, these instruments are shared by all children in the program. Wind instrument mouthpieces are sterilized with a disinfectant solution as each child finishes with them.

During the Exploratory Period, your child will try various instruments.

During the exploratory period each child learns to assemble the instruments and play a simple song on each of them. Since these instruments are owned by the school, parents don't have to buy or rent until an instrument is found that "fits" their child.

With some exploratory periods, children have to choose between band and orchestra before signing up. In other programs, children can try both band and stringed instruments before making a choice.

If your child has to choose before signing up, he may still be able to switch from band to strings, or vice versa, if he does so within the first couple of weeks after the exploratory period begins. The best part about the exploratory period is that your child gets to try various instruments and pick the one that he does best on.

Basic Orchestra Instruments

There are four basic orchestra (stringed) instruments — violin, viola, cello, and bass. Your child can probably start on any one of the four. The purpose of the exploratory period, then, will be to find out which one he likes best.

Stringed instruments come in different sizes for beginners. You can, for example, get a violin as small as $1/16$th the size of a standard instrument. Your child's orchestra teacher or your music dealer will help you choose the proper size instrument.

Basic Band Instruments

Basic band instruments for beginners include flute, clarinet, saxophone, cornet (trumpet), trombone, and percussion (snare drum and bells). Band instruments come only in full-size versions, so it is important that the instrument be fitted to your child, not vice versa.

This is why an exploratory period is so important. During the exploratory period your child gets to hold and play several different instruments, and if there are problems related to the size of the instrument, these problems can be recognized early on.

Special Band Instruments

Although beginners rarely start on them, there are some special band instruments which are typically owned by the school. The special instruments include: oboe, bassoon, bass clarinet, tenor and baritone saxophones, French horn, baritone horn, and tuba. Special instruments are ones that students usually switch to during junior high school (or middle school).

If getting an instrument from the school is the only way your child will be able to join band or orchestra, discuss this with the teacher early on. The teacher may be able to adjust the exploratory period to allow your child to try school-owned instruments.

There is no guarantee, of course, that your child will be able to play a school-owned instrument. The number of school-owned instruments is limited, and they are often handed out first to students who demonstrate unusual potential.

Three special instruments in particular — oboe, bassoon, and French horn — can be very tricky to learn. Most students who play these instruments find they need private lessons in addition to the class instruction they get at school. Obviously, if money is a problem, you may not want to consider one of these instruments.

If, however, you have talked with the band teacher because of a financial problem, or if your child has shown exceptional talent and the band teacher approaches you, one of these special instruments might be right for your child.

"Special" instruments include the oboe and the bassoon.

WHAT TO DO IF YOU ALREADY HAVE AN INSTRUMENT

If you have an instrument already, and it is in good repair, your child can probably start on that instrument, and you can save the cost of renting and buying later on.

There are a couple of caveats you should be aware of before starting your child on an instrument you already own.

Uncle Herb's Steel Clarinet

In my seventeen years as a public school music teacher, I have noticed that some children who bring a family-owned instrument to school are really bringing in a "home furnishing" that doesn't yet know it has passed on.

I am referring, of course, to Uncle Herb's Steel Clarinet. This is an instrument that has not been played since the end of Franklin Roosevelt's first term in office, and has been stored in the garage for almost fifty years. The case has taken on a musty odor, and the instrument itself ranges in hue from burnt orange to a dark moss green.

Despite warm family memories of Uncle Herb sitting around a crackling fire, playing polkas, this is not a musical instrument. It's either a valuable collector's item or a table lamp without a shade. In any case, don't force your child to play it.

The Wrong Instrument

Even if the instrument you own is in good condition, it may not be one your child does well on. If you have an instrument at home, you need to know whether your child will be able to play it. This is another area where the exploratory period can be a big help. If you have a saxophone, for example, and your child is able to play the clarinet during the exploratory period, the band teacher will know your child can be successful on your instrument.

If an exploratory period or other evaluation determines that this is not a good choice for your child, don't force the issue. Consider selling the instrument or saving it for another child. If you insist on starting your child on the wrong instrument, he will drop out. I can almost guarantee it.

Remember, in order for your child to be successful in band or orchestra, the key ingredients are *interest* and *support*. A child who is forced to play an instrument he has trouble making a sound on already has a built-in excuse for losing interest and quitting.

INSTRUMENTATION NEEDS OF THE BAND OR ORCHESTRA PROGRAM

The exploratory period isn't perfect. Guidance is still needed. String teachers don't want to end up with a room full of violins; band teachers all over the world have the same recurring nightmare in which they walk in the first day of class and are greeted by two hundred sixth graders — all holding tenor saxophones!

Sometimes so many children want to play a certain instrument, the instrumentation of the group gets out of balance. One of my first junior high school bands had sixty members in it. Of those sixty young musicians, twenty-five were drummers!

If there's a choice, encourage your child to start on a "needed" instrument. Photo by Tim Sams.

As a result, I had to "platoon" the percussion. That is, I organized the drummers into small groups (platoons) and only allowed one group to play at a time. If I had let them all play at once, the noise would have drowned out the sounds of all the other instruments.

If your child does well on more than one instrument during the exploratory period, find out the school's instrumentation needs from the band or orchestra teacher and encourage your child to start on one of the "needed" instruments. All other factors being equal, your child will get more attention and better instruction if he elects to play an instrument that the band or orchestra needs.

When you think about it, it's really not much different from a parent who encourages his child to try out for a certain position on an athletic team because that's where the need is. To combat instrumentation problems, some schools even have a quota system and allow only so many children to begin on certain instruments each year.

Balanced instrumentation is essential to a quality music program. After all, you can't have a football team with ten wide receivers and one guard; you can't have an orchestra with fifty violins and one viola; and you can't have a band with twenty-five drummers and . . . Well, you just can't have a band with twenty-five drummers!

WHY DOESN'T EVERYONE HAVE AN EXPLORATORY PERIOD?

"OK," you say. "This business of trying different instruments before choosing one sounds wonderful. If it's such a great idea, how come my child's school doesn't have an exploratory period?"

Good question.

Some schools don't feel they can afford even the modest inventory of school-owned instruments needed for an exploratory period. They may need to invest all available funds in "special" instruments — cellos, basses, oboes, bassoons, French horns, baritones, and tubas — instruments that parents don't normally buy.

Other schools may not have an exploratory period simply because no one has ever heard of it. Believe it or not, in most universities and colleges, a very small part of the time spent preparing to become a music teacher is spent talking about how to recruit beginners.

In my four years of undergraduate school, for example, I think we spent two whole class periods talking about recruiting students into band and orchestra. I didn't learn about using an exploratory period in college. I learned it from Clair Miller, a fellow teacher in the school district where I teach now, who developed the concept based on his association with other veteran teachers over the years. Frankly, most good teaching ideas are passed down like that, from one teacher to another, until soon it becomes standard practice.

If your child's school doesn't allow students to try different instruments before choosing, ask the teacher to consider doing it. I really believe it's the best way to start beginners in band and orchestra.

CREATING YOUR OWN EXPLORATORY PERIOD

If your school's beginning band or orchestra program doesn't offer an exploratory period, and the teacher isn't interested in starting one, there's a way you can create one — or a pretty fair substitute — on your own.

Go to a local music dealer and ask someone who is familiar with a variety of instruments to spend some time with your child, demonstrating the instruments and letting your child try them out.

Depending on the amount of competition among music dealers in your area, you may not have to pay for this time. An enterprising music dealer might figure he has a greater chance of selling you an instrument if he gets your child started on the right one to begin with. Even if you have to pay the standard "private lesson" rate, it will be worth it to find out which instrument your child is most likely to be successful on.

A word of caution: Don't expect a music dealer to provide your child with a full-blown seven or eight week exploratory period. You will be lucky if you get an hour, but that will still be better than the "squint" system or having your child pick an instrument based on the last Madonna video he saw on MTV.

ADAPTATION AND PHYSICAL TRAITS

With or without an exploratory period, you should know about some guidelines teachers use to help steer children away from potentially frustrating situations. These guidelines have to do with adaptation, or your child's physical makeup and its effect on the choice of an instrument. These are not hard and fast rules but simply guidelines to use in fine-tuning your child's final choice of an instrument.

- Children with small hands and fingers sometimes have trouble covering the holes on a clarinet. The same would be true for an "open holed" flute.
- Children with extremely short arms may have problems extending the slide on a trombone.
- Children with extremely uneven or sharp teeth may have difficulty playing clarinet or saxophone.
- Those with a decided overbite or front teeth that are widely spread apart may not do well on flute, clarinet, or saxophone.
- Children who cannot make a buzzing sound by pressing their lips together and blowing may have trouble playing brass instruments such as cornet or trombone.
- Since strings come in so many different sizes, most children can

play any of the four instruments. Some children, however, are too small to play even a down-size version of the two largest stringed instruments — cello and bass.

PROBLEMS OF ORTHODONTIA (BRACES)

Since orthodontia is a fact of life for so many children today, it deserves separate mention. If your child already has braces or will soon get them, you should discuss his interest in joining band or orchestra with your orthodontist — especially if your child wants to play a wind instrument.

Brasses, such as cornet or trombone, push the teeth inward. Woodwinds, like clarinet and saxophone, pull slightly outward on the upper teeth.

One woodwind instrument, the flute, doesn't put any direct pressure on the teeth, but sometimes braces interfere with forming the lips properly to make a good sound.

In most cases, orthodontal treatment can be adjusted to allow for the extra pressure of playing a wind instrument, and your child can continue to play the instrument of his choice without problems.

Your orthodontist can provide "orthodontic wax" to protect against discomfort. A new product called Brace-Guard® consists of two materials which, when mixed together, form a shield that can be used over and over to protect lips from cuts and irritation. Ask your child's orthodontist what he recommends.

In certain circumstances, where the malformation of the teeth is severe, your child's orthodontist may recommend against playing a wind instrument.

There are, unfortunately, orthodontists who say *no* child should play a wind instrument while undergoing orthodontia. If your orthodontist falls into that category you have two choices: (1) you can eliminate wind instruments for your child; (2) you can find another orthodontist who is willing to make adjustments in your child's treatment.

Even if playing a wind instrument is out of the question for your child, there are still the four stringed instruments and percussion to choose from. Chances are your child can find an instrument that he can play and will be happy with.

EXCEPTIONAL LEARNERS

The law — Public Law 94-142, to be precise — says that all children must be provided with a "free and appropriate public education in the least restrictive environment . . ."

Children with Physical, Emotional, and Mental Handicaps

One of the results of the passing of PL 94-142 has been the "mainstreaming" of handicapped youngsters into certain school environments, among these music, including band and orchestra. Whether your handicapped youngster will be able to join band or orchestra depends on your local school district's interpretation of the term "least restrictive environment."

I can't interpret the law, and considering my driving habits, you probably wouldn't want me to! Besides, individual circumstances in each school district often dictate what programs can be made available for the mainstreaming of handicapped children. What I *can* do is share with you my experiences in dealing with exceptional children in instrumental performance groups and offer some suggestions, should your child decide to join band or orchestra.

Over the years, I have taught a number of handicapped students — some with visual and hearing impairments; others who were emotionally disturbed or who had physical handicaps; and some who were mentally retarded.

In most cases, these exceptional children, through exceptional effort, were able to learn to play a band or orchestra instrument and function as a member of the school group. Some of the most rewarding experiences I have had as a teacher have been the result of being able to work with students who overcame great odds to achieve success in music.

I once had a high school musician whose hearing impairment was so severe, he heard less than 10% of the sounds "normal" people hear. He actually played clarinet in concert and marching band and kept time by taking visual cues from those around him or by feeling vibrations through his bare feet on the floor!

Another student learned to hold a cornet with his withered

arm and became one of the top musicians in band.

Still another youngster, who was classified EMR (Educable Mentally Retarded), took private lessons twice a week and practiced an hour a day, seven days a week, in order to keep up with the rest of the class. Despite all the hard work, in three years of high school, this student never moved up more than one or two chairs from the bottom of her section. Yet, at her high school graduation, she came up to me and said band had been her favorite class and that she would never forget the time she spent there.

There are many youngsters, like the ones I have mentioned, in bands and orchestras today — children who want nothing more than a chance to be part of something "normal." Their dedication and willingness to work hard for success are often inspiring to all members of the group. Most band and orchestra teachers I know go out of their way to help handicapped children fit into their performing groups.

Talk with the band or orchestra teacher about your child's interest in learning to play an instrument. Be honest about your child's abilities and ask the teacher to be honest with you regarding his feelings about your child's chances for success in band or orchestra.

Mainstreaming handicapped children is fairly new for many band and orchestra teachers. Most of us have very little formal training in dealing with exceptional learners and we are often not sure how a child's handicap will affect his chances for success.

If your child does join band or orchestra, be prepared, as always, to offer lots of encouragement and help. And don't expect miracles. Your child may be last chair for as long as he is a member of the band or orchestra. Remember, "mainstreaming" your handicapped child into a performance group puts him in competition with other children whose skill levels may be higher.

With proper guidance, however, your child can learn how to play an instrument, and his experience as a member of an instrumental performing group will probably be one of the highlights of his years in school.

Gifted and Talented Children

Most people don't think of "gifted" children as having a handicap. However, a high degree of creativity or intelligence can result in so many problems in school that the "gifted" child can barely function. It isn't unusual for gifted students to do poorly in some subjects or even fail certain classes.

Your gifted child may discover that joining the band or orchestra becomes a creative outlet that allows him to be part of a group and at the same time use abilities that have, up to this point, made him feel strange and out of place.

This is not to say that you can simply shove your talented youngster into band or orchestra and forget him. He will still be exceptional, even in a music performance group. Most of the other children in band and orchestra will be "average" in ability and creativity but, in this case, your child might become a leader rather than an "outcast."

One way for your gifted child to be a leader, if he decides to join band, is for him to play one of the special instruments, such as oboe, bassoon, or French horn. As stated earlier, these instruments are often school-owned and loaned to selected students at a very nominal fee. This doesn't get you off the hook financially, however. Even for a gifted child, a special instrument can be a challenge, often requiring private study in order for the child to be successful.

Private lessons can not only help your child achieve success but can provide the challenge a gifted youngster often needs later on.

RECAP

- Choosing the right instrument is critical to your child's success in band or orchestra.
- Your child's choice of an instrument will determine whether he will be in band or orchestra.
- Don't allow your child to choose an instrument without discussing it with the band or orchestra teacher.
- The best way to choose an instrument is through an exploratory period in which your child tries several different instruments over an extended period of time.
- School-owned instruments are sometimes available for talented beginners or when there is a financial problem.
- If you already own an instrument and your child has shown he can handle it, you can save money by letting your child play it.

- Take the instrumentation needs of the band or orchestra into account when choosing an instrument.
- You can create your own exploratory period by asking for help from your local music dealer.
- Orthodontia can be adjusted to allow your child to play just about any wind instrument.
- If there are severe problems with teeth and mouth formation, choose a stringed instrument or percussion.
- Exceptional children — those with physical, emotional, and mental handicaps — can be successful in band or orchestra.
- Gifted children are often candidates for special instruments including oboe, bassoon, and French horn.

The purpose of this chapter is to help you and your child make a choice of an instrument. Keep in mind, however, that if you follow all the suggestions, take every precaution, and even cross your fingers, mistakes happen.

If your child discovers, after a few weeks, that the instrument he chose is not the one he *really* wants to play, discuss it with the band or orchestra teacher. It may not be necessary for your child to drop out. Early on, a change of instruments is often possible.

Next step: Getting the instrument!

3.

GETTING AN INSTRUMENT

After your child has chosen the instrument he wants to play in band or orchestra, it's your job to get one. For the parent who has never been through the process of buying or renting a musical instrument, that experience alone can be traumatic!

GOING SHOPPING — NIGHT OF THE LIVING DREAD

You arrive at the address listed in the phone book and open the door. It's quiet inside, almost like a doctor's office. "This is strange," you think. "Shouldn't someone be singing or playing an instrument? Where's the Muzak?"

The man who greets you is nice enough, but there's something about him that frightens you. Maybe it's the fact that he looks a little like an undertaker. "Aren't music dealers happy?" you ask yourself.

Then there are all those instruments — thousands of dollars worth of gleaming, handcrafted metal and wood sculptures, inside glass cases, almost as if they were on display in an art museum.

"Something's not right," you mutter under your breath. "I can't quite put my finger on it, but for some reason I feel apprehensive."

Suddenly you realize the problem. You left the house to go on a simple shopping trip and ended up in the Musical Twilight Zone. You know where you are, but you don't know what you want!

The truth is, there's no reason to feel intimidated. Getting your child's first instrument is a simple business transaction, like buying a vacuum cleaner. Well, not exactly like buying a vacuum cleaner. It's more like buying a stereo.

Actually, it's not like that either. Because, at first you aren't going to buy anything. The first thing you will do is rent. Let me explain.

RENT FIRST, BUY LATER

Unless there is some compelling reason to buy, you should rent your child's instrument for at least the first three months.

Most orchestra beginners start on a down-size (less than full-size) instrument, so there's no reason to buy until the child is able to play a full-size instrument. Music dealers who specialize in stringed instruments allow you to change instruments as often as necessary until your child is able to play a full-size one.

Band instruments come only in full-size versions, so you do not have to worry about your child changing instruments. Most beginners in band, though, also rent at first. This is to prevent parents from spending hundreds of dollars on an instrument, only to have their child drop out of band.

A typical rental period is three months. After the initial rental period you will have the option of buying or continuing to rent. Almost all music stores will apply your rental to the purchase of an instrument. Some even have "rent to own" programs in which you rent the instrument until it is paid for.

INSTRUMENT TYPES: STUDENT LINE TO PROFESSIONAL

Band and orchestra instruments fit into one of three quality categories: "Student Line"; "Intermediate"; and "Professional."

Without going into a lot of detail here (I'll do that in Chapter 7), suffice it to say your child should probably start on a "student line" instrument.

Since most music dealers rent only student line instruments, you probably won't have a choice. Student line instruments are made for beginners. They are a little sturdier and are designed to handle the occasional mishap that beginners sometimes bestow on them.

NEW OR USED — WHICH SHOULD I GET?

String dealers typically have instruments that are used only for rental. You can't buy them even if you want to. When your child is ready for a full-size instrument, you can buy "new" or "old" (again, these differences will be discussed more fully in Chapter 7).

Most band instrument dealers rent new instruments, which they hope you will buy at the conclusion of the rental period. Many also offer "pre-owned" or "pre-rented" instruments, which can also be purchased at the end of the rental period.

The main distinction between band and strings is that string dealers maintain separate rental-only instruments; band instrument dealers sell what they rent.

The cost of renting will probably be the same, whether you rent new or used. All your rental applies to purchase anyway, and you will realize the difference between new and used when you buy.

To sum up: With strings there is no choice — you rent whatever is available. With band instruments, your decision should be based on whether you plan to buy a new or used instrument at the conclusion of the rental period.

GUARANTEED BUY-BACK — ONE REASON TO PURCHASE UP FRONT

Some dealers offer a "guaranteed buy-back" plan. With this plan, you buy up front instead of renting. If your child quits within an agreed upon period of time, usually three months, you can return the instrument and get all your money back — minus a pro-rated rental fee.

The incentive for you to do this is a hefty discount off the list price if you buy up front. The discount can amount to around 30%

off list ($135 off the price of a $450 instrument). Guaranteed buy-back plans usually apply only to new instruments.

HOW MUCH DOES IT COST TO RENT?

Monthly rental of most student line instruments costs any-where from $12 to $25, depending on the type of instrument and the cost of insurance to cover damage, loss, and theft.

For stringed instruments, violin and viola rent for about the same amount, cello is about twice as much as violin, and bass is twice the cost of cello rental. In many school districts, cellos and basses are owned by the school, so beginners don't have to rent them from a store anyway.

Of the basic band instruments, flute, clarinet, cornet, trom-bone, and drums all cost about the same to rent. Saxophones are about twice the amount charged for the other basic instruments. Most special instruments (oboe, bassoon, French horn) can't be rented from a music store. (This isn't usually a problem, since, like cellos and basses, most schools have their own special instru-ments.)

Your rental payments, minus the cost of insurance, accumu-late and are deducted from the selling price when you buy the in-strument. Typically, all rent paid is deducted when you buy, no matter how long you rent.

BUYING AFTER THE INITIAL RENTAL PERIOD

After the initial rental period, you will be given the opportu-nity to buy the instrument. A discount will be offered, but it will not be as much as the one you would have gotten for buying up front.

If you choose to buy at this time, most stores offer a financing plan to spread out the payments over several months. Some stores do their own financing and don't charge as much interest as a bank would. Some don't charge a finance charge at all.

RENTING TO OWN

Many dealers will allow you to continue renting the instrument until it's paid for. If you do this, you probably won't get a discount and will end up paying full list price for the instrument. You can, of course, return the instrument at any time during the rental period, and have no further obligation.

STRINGS ARE DIFFERENT

You will rent a stringed instrument until your child is ready for a full-size instrument. At that time you can buy a new full-size student line instrument or you can buy a "step up" model — one a little better than student line. The point to remember is that you probably won't buy the instrument you have been renting, but your rental payments will still apply to purchase. Many string students buy a "step up" model when they get to full size, rather than a student line instrument.

You will rent a down-size string instrument until your child is ready for full-size.

INSURANCE

Most rental plans offer damage and theft insurance. In most cases, stores underwrite their own plans, which, typically, run from $3 to $5 a month.

I strongly urge you to get whatever insurance or maintenance plan is offered by the music dealer. Instrument insurance is not expensive and you really can't afford to be without it.

Find out whether any insurance offered covers lost or stolen instruments. While your homeowner's policy will probably cover theft, you may have a rather large deductible.

WHERE TO SHOP

Since most student-line instruments are rented before they are purchased, many are obtained from local music dealers. Chances are, that's where you will go to get your child's first instrument. The local music dealer has a lot going for him and, in most instances, is the best place for you to get an instrument.

Local Music Stores

If you plan to rent an instrument, the logical place to go is a local music dealer. A local store will know how your school's band and orchestra program operates and will probably stock the beginning band or orchestra method book your child's teacher prefers.

In many cases a service representative from the local dealer calls on your child's school on a regular basis. And the local dealer is as handy as a phone call or short drive away in the event of a problem.

Finally, the local dealer probably offers instrument repair right at the store. The combination of an affordable rental plan, service, convenience, and in-store repair makes the local dealer a good choice for most people.

Depending on the size of your community, you may have several music stores to choose from. If your school has a music store come in to demonstrate instruments for beginners, you are not obligated to get your instrument from that store. If there are several stores in your area, you might want to shop around.

If you are considering renting or buying an instrument from a store that doesn't service your child's school, you should ask the band or orchestra teacher about that store. Some stores handle band and orchestra instruments as a sideline rather than as a main part of their business. These stores sometimes rent and sell inferior quality instruments.

There are alternatives to a local music store if you aren't close to one, or if, for some reason, you choose not to deal with a local store.

Mail Order

In recent years a number of music mail order catalog companies have sprung up. Most are reputable businesses, and many are able to undercut the price of local music stores due to lower overhead costs. Even when you figure in the cost of shipping, mail order dealers are usually less expensive than the initial cost of doing business with a local store.

How much less expensive? Local music dealers usually say they can come within 15 to 20% of the price offered by mail order catalogs. It's up to you to decide if the services provided by the local music dealer are worth the added cost of doing business locally.

If you live in an area where there is no local music dealer, or if, for some reason, you choose not to deal with one, a mail order catalog is an alternative you might want to consider.

Appendix D lists several mail order music dealers. You can call or write and ask them to send you a catalog. Some of them even rent instruments and, though they aren't as convenient as a local dealer, most do handle major name brand instruments.

One of the big problems of dealing with a mail order dealer is that to a parent with limited knowledge about music instruments, a mail order music catalog might read like the "Assembly Instructions for Stonehenge."

One obvious source of advice before doing business with a mail order dealer is your child's band or orchestra teacher. Most teachers are familiar with the major national mail order dealers and, more important, they will be able to advise you about the choice of a name brand instrument for your child.

Another thing you need to consider before doing business with a mail order catalog is repair. Warranty service is performed by the "selling dealer." This means that if you buy an instrument from a catalog, you can't take it to a local dealer for warranty service. You will have to pack it up, ship it to the catalog dealer, and wait for them to repair the instrument and send it back.

Though most major catalog mail order music dealers are members of their local Better Business Bureau and are interested in providing good service to you, the mail order business does have its share of crooks and dishonest people. If you decide to buy or rent from a catalog, make sure you know exactly what you are getting and where to go in the event of a problem.

Private Seller/Want Ads

I don't recommend getting an instrument from a private seller or from want ads without the help of your child's music teacher or some other knowledgeable person. Frequently the band or orchestra teacher will know of individuals who have instruments for sale. The typical selling price for used student line instruments is about one-fourth the cost of a new instrument ($100 to $150).

If the instrument is less than a year old and in immaculate condition, the seller will often try to get more. You can probably buy a "rental return" with a new warranty from a music dealer about as cheap as you can buy a one-year-old instrument from a private seller.

Another thing to consider is that used instruments purchased from private sellers have often been stored in a closet or attic for several years. Pads may have deteriorated, wood may have cracked, and slides may have corroded.

Keep in mind, also, that buying a used instrument from a private seller is like buying a used car from an individual. Unless your child's teacher or someone who knows something about musical instruments provides advice, you might get taken.

Some parents rent a new instrument for three months from a music dealer, then buy a used instrument from a private seller. When they do this, they lose the rental they have paid the store, but sometimes the cheaper cost of the used instrument makes it worthwhile.

Before you do this, however, check with the music dealer about buying a trade-in at the end of the rental period. The trade-in will probably cost more from the dealer than you could buy it from an individual, but it will be in good playing condition, it will include some kind of warranty and, better still, the store will probably apply at least part of the rent you paid toward the purchase price of the used instrument.

If you decide to buy from a private seller, make sure your child's teacher or an independent repair person looks at the instrument and tells you if it needs any repair.

Renting from the School

In some school districts beginners can rent instruments from the school. In this case, I'm talking about regular student line instruments, not the special instruments. In some school orchestra programs, for example, parents can rent stringed instruments for as long as their child is in school. In a few places, even band instruments are available. Other schools have a limited number of instruments and rent or loan them to children in families where there is a demonstrated financial need.

Some schools offer instruments to all children during the exploratory period — or initial three months — then expect parents to get an instrument after that time. If your school district has regular student line instruments available for rental, they will probably tell you this when your child signs up for band or orchestra.

WATCH OUT FOR INFERIOR INSTRUMENTS

No matter where you go to rent or buy your instrument, you need to be on the lookout for cheap, imitation, "off brand" instruments, especially those made in Taiwan. These instruments are mass-produced pieces of junk, manufactured by companies out to make a quick buck.

The instruments are so poorly constructed, reputable repair shops won't touch them. Furthermore, parts are not available or take months to arrive from the manufacturer.

How can you tell whether an instrument is an "off brand"? Stick with one of the major instrument brands listed in the next section or ask your child's music teacher.

MAJOR MANUFACTURERS AND DISTRIBUTORS

Below is a list of some of the major name brand student line instruments. This is not meant to be an all-inclusive list, and if you

STRINGED INSTRUMENTS Violin, Viola, Cello, Bass	WOODWINDS Flute, Clarinet, Saxophone
Glaesel International Strings Juzek Knilling Wm. Lewis J. Lidi Meisel Schroetter N. Suzuki	Amati Armstrong Artley Blessing Buffet Bundy Conn Gemeinhardt LeBlanc Noblet Normandy Olds Reynolds Selmer Signet Vito Yamaha
BRASSES **Cornet/Trumpet,** **Trombone**	**PERCUSSION** **(Drums)**
Bach Benge Besson Blessing Bundy Conn DEG Getzen Holton King Olds Yamaha	Ludwig Olds Pearl Ross Yamaha

come across a brand not listed, ask your child's teacher about it before you rent or buy.

Special instruments are not included since they are usually already owned by the school. If, for some reason, you do decide to buy your child one of the special instruments, you should ask for help from the music teacher or a private instructor.

GETTING THE BEST PRICE

Use the Instrument Price Comparison Sheet in Appendix A to record cost and rental information from all the stores or mail order catalogs you contact.

On the first line, record the name of the music dealer or mail order catalog. Then write down the phone number and the name of the person you talk with on the phone.

On the "Instrument" line, indicate which instrument you are getting information about, i.e., flute, clarinet, violin, viola. On the next line write down the brand or model number your child's teacher prefers. If your child's teacher doesn't have a preference, write down the manufacturer and model name the salesman quotes you a price on.

Circle the word "New" or the word "Used," depending on whether you are being quoted a price on a brand new or pre-rented/owned instrument. The salesman may tell you that it will depend on availability when you come into the store. If he does, ask for information about a new instrument, since that will be the most you would pay.

Write down the price of the instrument if you bought it up front. This price should include some sort of discount (usually 25 to 30% off list price). Ask about a guaranteed buy-back.

Next, you want to find out the price after the initial rental period (usually three months). If the store offers a discount for buying any time beyond the initial rental, find out when (after how many months) and how much the discount is.

Write down the monthly rental amount. Don't include the cost of maintenance or insurance in this figure. Find out whether your rental payments will apply to the purchase of the instrument. Then get the cost of insurance or maintenance per month and record that figure.

If you are interested, ask about financing. Be sure to get the annual percentage rate (APR). Your monthly payment, of course, will depend on the amount you finance, so that figure may not be readily available. It's really not important at this point, but write it down if it is offered.

You will want to know if the store has its own repair shop or if instruments are sent out for repair. You will also want to know whether loaner instruments are provided. Typically, loaners are only offered when the repair will take more than a week or two.

Write down any notes or unusual facts about the store in the "Notes" section.

Fill out the Instrument Price Comparison Sheet for each of the stores you contact.

I suggest phoning rather than visiting in person. You can cover more ground more easily; you can fill out your form without feeling stupid; and you will not be subject to pressure to rent on the spot.

If you are interested in contacting any of the mail order dealers, call or write for a catalog, or call and get the information you need. (Several major mail order dealers are listed in Appendix D.) The mail order dealer's catalog will provide details of their rental program (if any), repair facilities, and most other information you will need. Most mail order dealers carry more brands and models of instruments than are listed in their catalog. If you are interested in the price of a specific brand or model, you might have to call for that information.

A word on instrument brands and models: Unless your child's teacher states a preference for a certain brand and model of instrument, make sure you stick with a known, major manufacturer and get a student line instrument. Each of us has developed our preferences over the years, but as long as the instrument is made by one of the major manufacturers, any student line instrument will be acceptable.

Ask the dealer to show you and your child how to assemble the instrument.

FINALLY — GETTING THE INSTRUMENT

Using the information you gathered on the Instrument Price Comparison Sheet, you can decide where you want to get your child's instrument.

If you go to a local dealer, take your child with you. When you get the instrument, ask the dealer to show you and your child how to assemble and disassemble it. If your child had an exploratory period at school, he will probably already know how to do this, but it helps to have the dealer show you as well.

Make sure you get everything you need, including your child's first method book, if required. Most stores provide necessary accessories with rental instruments. Your child's teacher will probably send home a letter or note telling you what you need to get along with the instrument.

The list of needed items should include: rosin for stringed instruments, reeds for woodwinds, oil for brasses, and sticks and mallets for percussion.

If you don't have one, be sure to get a folding music stand.

Your child will not develop good playing habits if he has to practice at home by propping his music on a pillow and sitting on the edge of his bed.

If you get your instrument from a mail order catalog, you won't be able to get help assembling the instrument. You might be able to visit the school and get help from your child's teacher. I really believe every parent should know how to assemble and disassemble their child's instrument. After all, you are the one who will supervise him at home and if you don't know what he should be doing, chances are something will go wrong.

RECAP

- Rent at first, unless the dealer offers a guaranteed buy-back. All rent paid should apply to purchase.
- It is usually best to rent or buy from a local music dealer. Other sources for instruments include: mail order catalogs, private sellers, and school-owned instruments.
- Monthly rental runs between $12 and $25.
- Make sure your rent includes damage and theft insurance.
- Watch out for "off brand" instruments made in Taiwan. Stick with known major manufacturers.
- Use the price comparison form in Appendix A when shopping for an instrument to rent or buy. Shop around and compare prices from several stores if possible.
- Make sure you get everything you need with the instrument.
- Ask the dealer to show you and your child how to put the instrument together and how to take it apart.

After getting the instrument, your child needs to know how to take care of it. And you need to know what to do in case there is a problem.

The answers are only a page away.

4.

WARRANTIES
AND MAINTENANCE

Your child must be taught, from the very beginning, that his new instrument is not a toy. It is an expensive, finely crafted tool for making music. Whether student line or professional quality, your child's instrument has been made according to exacting standards with very small tolerances between moving parts. Often, even a slight amount of mis-handling can cause extensive damage.

MANUFACTURER WARRANTIES

Manufacturer warranties on musical instruments cover defects in workmanship or materials and are serviced by the "selling dealer." This means that if you have a problem with your child's instrument, you must take it to the dealer where you bought it for repair or service.

If you buy the instrument from a local music dealer, that should be no problem. If, however, you purchase your instrument from a mail order catalog, this will probably mean packing the instrument up and shipping it (often at your expense) to the selling catalog dealer.

In addition to warranting that the instrument, including all parts, is free from defects in materials and workmanship, manufacturer warranties typically provide the following kinds of protection:

Violin, Viola, Cello, Bass	Plastic Clarinet
❏ One year warranty against seams opening. ❏ No warranty on finish deterioration. ❏ Strings, bridge, bow, pegs, tailpiece hangar, and soundpost not warranted.	❏ Five year warranty on plastic body. ❏ Springs, pads, felt parts, corks, tuning barrel, bell, mouthpiece, and reeds not warranted.
Wood Clarinet	**Flute, Saxophone, Cornet, Trumpet, Trombone, Percussion**
❏ Six to twelve month warranty against cracking. ❏ Springs, pads, felt parts, corks, tuning barrel, bell, mouthpiece, and reeds not warranted.	❏ One year warranty on most parts. ❏ No warranty on finish. ❏ Springs, pads, felt parts, corks, mouthpiece, and reeds not warranted.

Most dealers support the manufacturer warranty by going a step further. Typically, a music dealer will cover just about *any* problem with an instrument for up to a year. This means that if something goes wrong and it's not strictly covered by the manufacturer, the dealer will probably take care of it.

The music business is one of the few industries where this happens, which is probably why most music dealers I know don't make very much money!

INSURANCE

While you are renting an instrument, you will probably be offered some sort of combination insurance and maintenance coverage. This covers just about anything that can happen to the instrument and is not expensive.

After you buy, the loss or theft of your instrument will be covered under your homeowner's policy as long as the instrument is not used to earn money. If the instrument is used professionally, you will probably have to obtain a separate rider on your policy.

Your homeowner's policy may have a rather large deductible. Check with your insurance agent if you are not sure. You may want to consider a separate musical instrument policy. (See Appendix E for companies that provide instrument insurance.)

MAINTENANCE

After the manufacturer and dealer warranties expire, maintenance and repair are your responsibility. In general, the repair of a musical instrument is best left to the experts — instrument repair technicians and violin makers.

Get the Instrument Checked Twice a Year

According to the experts mentioned above, the most important thing you can do to protect your investment in a musical instrument is to have it checked out twice a year. Most repair technicians will check your child's instrument for a nominal fee. If minor adjustments are needed, they can often be done while you wait.

Have your child's instrument checked out by the dealer or a repair technician twice a year.

Have the instrument checked at the end of the school year and one time during the year — about halfway through. This simple twice a year checkup will, according to professional repairmen, eliminate 90% of the problems you might encounter later on.

Daily Maintenance

One of the most common causes of instrument damage — Little Brother using Big Brother's trombone as a shoulder-fired rocket launcher in the annual children's reenactment of *Rambo Takes on Communism* — can easily be avoided.

More damage is caused by children leaving an instrument lying on the bedroom floor and forgetting about it than just about anything else. When your child is not practicing or playing his instrument, it should be kept in its case. Children often get in a hurry when they finish practicing and don't take care of their instrument properly unless someone makes sure they do. One important piece of advice then, that applies to all musical instruments, is this: *Don't allow your child to leave his instrument unattended!*

In terms of maintenance, there are some basic daily care tips your child should follow. Go over these with your child and supervise until you are sure he is doing it on his own.

Strings

Stringed instruments are made of wood, so they need the same care any fine wood demands. Your child's stringed instrument should not be stored or kept in extreme environments — too damp, too dry, too hot, or too cold.

Excessive dryness can cause splitting or seam separation, necessitating expensive repair. A simple sponge-like device called a Dampit® fits into the F hole and can help maintain proper humidity. A Dampit® costs between $5 and $10, depending on size, and includes a humidity indicator which can be left in the case with the instrument, telling you when you need to use the Dampit®.

Rosin, which is applied to the bow to provide friction, leaves a deposit on the instrument. This deposit can be picked up with a treated cleaning cloth. Also available is a variety of cleaners and polishes which are safe to use on the fine varnished finish of a stringed instrument.

Cellos and basses have a peg (endpin) which rests on the floor in a disk-shaped protector and prevents the instrument from sliding across the floor while being played. Peg compound allows pegs to turn easily and prevents slipping and sticking.

Strings are held in place under tension. Don't allow your child to loosen the strings, or else the bridge, on which the strings rest, may fall off. Also, the soundpost, a small wooden rod inside the instrument, may fall over. If the bridge or soundpost does come loose, the instrument must be taken to the orchestra teacher or a repair shop. You can't reset a bridge or soundpost yourself.

Bows have a screw for adjusting the tension of the bow hair. Tension should be loosened before the bow is put away.

Flute

A cleaning rod is included with the flute, and a small, soft, clean cloth attached to the end of the rod can be drawn through the joints to wipe out moisture. Shake excess water out of the head joint, then dry the inside of the head joint with the cloth on the cleaning rod. All connecting joints should be wiped inside and out, and each section of the flute should be wiped with a soft, clean cloth to keep the finish clean.

Most teachers discourage students from using key oil. Children tend to overdo it and the excess oil attracts dirt, causing more harm than good. Before buying or using key oil, ask your child's teacher for advice.

Never use silver polish on a flute. It contains abrasives that cause damage to the finish.

Oboe

Remove the reed and blow the moisture out of it before putting it in its case. Carefully disassemble the instrument and swab the joints with a cleaning feather or oboe swab.

Put the protective caps over the corks before putting the joints in the case.

Most teachers discourage students from using key oil. Before buying or using key oil, ask your child's teacher for advice.

Never use silver polish on oboe keys.

Bassoon

Remove the reed and blow the water out of it before returning it to its case. Shake the water out of the bocal and blow on one end to remove excess moisture.

Carefully disassemble the instrument and swab out the top joints with a bassoon swab before returning the parts to the case.

Empty excess water from the boot joint before returning it to the case.

Clarinet

The reed should never be left on the mouthpiece. After playing, it should be removed, excess moisture wiped off, and the reed stored in a holder.

The mouthpiece should be wiped out and swabbed with a soft clean cloth, then each of the joints should be swabbed out with a clarinet swab and the tenons (joint ends) wiped off.

Most teachers discourage students from using key oil. Before buying or using key oil, ask your child's teacher for advice.

Never use silver polish on clarinet keys.

Saxophone

The reed should never be left on the mouthpiece. After playing, it should be removed, excess moisture wiped off, and stored in a reed holder.

The mouthpiece should be wiped out and swabbed with a soft clean cloth. Then the neck should be removed and swabbed with a neck cleaner. Finally, a weighted saxophone swab should be dropped into the bell and drawn through the body.

The outside of the saxophone can be wiped with a soft, clean cloth or a treated cleaning cloth.

Most teachers discourage students from using key oil. Before buying or using key oil, ask your child's teacher for advice.

Never use metal polish on a saxophone.

Cornet/Trumpet

The valves must be oiled with trumpet valve oil before each use. Other types of oil such as 3-in-1 will not do, because they are much too thick. The problem with beginners oiling the valves is that they take out the valves, drop them on the floor, then put them in backward. Here's a way to oil the valves without taking them out.

1. Depress the first valve and keep it down while pulling out the slide that leads to that valve.

2. Place a few drops of oil into one of the tubes leading to the first valve.

3. Replace the slide, keeping the valve pressed down.

4. Rapidly move all three valves up and down to distribute the oil. Later on, your child's teacher can show him how to oil the valves by removing them one at a time.

All slides must be kept greased. Tuning slide grease is available for this.

There is a water key or spit valve used to empty water that accumulates in the instrument from your child's saliva. Emptying the spit valve can get kind of messy, but if your child doesn't do it, pretty soon he sounds like he is playing under water. Have him use the bathroom or a waste basket. You can also put a rag or several pieces of paper towel on the floor.

The instrument can be wiped off with a soft, clean cloth. A treated cleaning cloth can also be used.

Never use metal polish on a trumpet or cornet.

French Horn

The valves must be oiled with rotary valve oil before each use. Other types of oil such as 3-in-1 will not do, because they are much too thick.

To oil the valves:

1. Depress the first valve and keep it down while pulling out the slide that leads to that valve.

2. Place a few drops of oil into one of the tubes leading to the first valve.

3. Replace the slide, keeping the valve pressed down.

4. Rapidly move all three valves up and down to distribute the oil. Later on, your child's teacher can show him how to oil the valves separately.

All slides must be kept greased. Tuning slide grease is available for this.

There is no water key on the French horn. To empty water, the instrument must be carefully rotated (bell over mouthpiece) at least twice to allow water to empty from the lead pipe. Watch out. The water will come out when you least expect it!

You will notice that there are "strings" on the valves of the French horn. If one comes loose or breaks, the valve won't work. Don't try to re-string it yourself. It takes a special kind of string and is best done by a repairman or the teacher. As your child gets older he will learn how to do it himself, but it's not a job for a beginner.

The instrument can be wiped off with a soft, clean cloth. A treated cleaning cloth can also be used.

Never use metal polish on a French horn.

Trombone

The slide must be oiled before each use. Most beginners use trombone slide oil or liquid trombone slide cream. Later on, your child's teacher might show him to use the slide cream and water bottle technique, but this is usually too complicated for beginners. Besides, it puts a "water squirter" in the hands of an adolescent, which, as far as I'm concerned, is a strict violation of the Parent's Law of Common Sense!

To oil the slide:

1. Rest the tip of the slide on the floor.

2. Unlock the slide.

3. Lift the instrument about a foot, exposing a section of the inner slide.

4. Place several drops of oil or liquid cream on both sections of the inner slide.

5. Move the slide up and down rapidly.

The tuning slide must be kept greased. Tuning slide grease is available for this.

The water key or spit valve should be emptied regularly. Use the bathroom, a wastebasket, or keep a rag or several pieces of paper towel on the floor.

The outside of the instrument can be wiped off with a soft, clean cloth, or a treated cleaning cloth can be purchased.

Never use metal polish on a trombone.

Percussion

The drum heads or bells should be cleaned regularly with a damp cloth.

Never pluck the snares on the bottom of the snare drum.

Only proper drum sticks or mallets should be used to play the snare drum or bell unit.

LEAVE REPAIR TO THE EXPERTS

There is almost no repair you or your child can do on a musical instrument. Most band and orchestra teachers will help with minor problems, but we don't even like to do much beyond removing stuck mouthpieces and oiling valves.

Do not try to reset bridges or soundposts on stringed instruments, remove stuck mouthpieces or slides on brass instruments, or replace loose pads on woodwinds. Leave that stuff to the experts.

A favorite pastime of music teachers at conventions is telling "Dad Fixed My Instrument" stories.

One day, during my first year of teaching, one of my best junior high clarinet players came to band in tears.

"Mr. P.," she sobbed, "I'm gonna have to quit band because my dad tried to fix my clarinet."

I told her things couldn't be that bad. "What did your dad do to your clarinet?" I asked.

"He tried to put one of the pads back on."

"Did he use his cigarette lighter?" I asked. (A common problem with parents trying to fix clarinets is that they don't realize a cigarette lighter puts out too big a flame for this kind of job.)

"No, he didn't use his cigarette lighter."

"What DID he use?"

"His blowtorch."

It turns out Dad was a welder. He didn't use his arc welder, but he did use a propane torch on the plastic clarinet, which, in this case, was a little like trying to start up a charcoal grill with napalm!

The tearful young musician showed me her instrument. It's difficult to describe in words, but if you can, just picture what a bolt of lightning would do to a blacksnake.

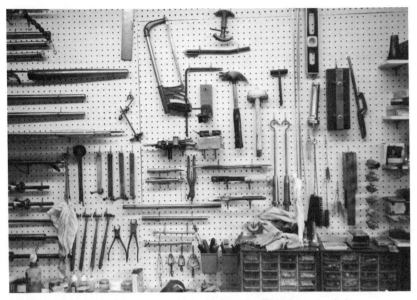

Repairing an instrument takes special tools. This is not a job for the family handyman.

She didn't have to quit band, but her parents did have to buy her a new instrument. I think they made a table lamp out of the blacksnake.

The moral is: When your child's instrument needs repair, take it to an expert. Don't try to fix it yourself. Unless you really need a new table lamp.

CHOOSING A REPAIR TECHNICIAN

There are no licensing procedures for instrument repair technicians. Anyone who wants to can open an instrument repair shop. There are, however, some things you can do to ensure you are dealing with a reputable repairman.

First of all, talk with your child's music teacher. Teachers know who the good repair people are. No repair technician can survive long if he doesn't build a good reputation among school music teachers.

Second, look for someone who belongs to one of the two main professional organizations for repair technicians.

NAPBIRT members exchange information on instrument repair and receive updates from manufacturers.

Professional Associations for Repair Technicians

The National Association of Professional Band Instrument Repair Technicians (NAPBIRT) was founded in 1976 as a non-profit, international, self-governing organization, dedicated to technical integrity and professionalism in the craft of repair, restoration, and maintenance of band instruments.

Members of NAPBIRT sponsor and attend seminars and regularly exchange information on instrument repair. NAPBIRT has an excellent relationship with major band instrument manufacturers, and NAPBIRT members receive updates regarding new developments in the field.

If you have a problem with a repair done by a NAPBIRT member, you can contact NAPBIRT's council of professional practices. (The address and phone number is in Appendix E.)

The American Federation of Violin and Bow Makers (AFVBM) is the professional association for experts in the making, restoring, and repairing of stringed instruments. (See Appendix E for address and phone number.) As with NAPBIRT, you can contact AFVBM if you have a problem with a member regarding repair of your child's stringed instrument.

Membership in NAPBIRT (for band instrument repair technicians) and AFVBM (for violin makers) is voluntary. These are professional associations, not licensing agencies, so they don't have any legal authority.

If you seek recommendations from your child's teacher or deal only with members of these two organizations, you will probably be all right when it comes to repair of your child's instrument.

RECAP

- Warranty work is done by the selling dealer.
- Your homeowner's policy will provide insurance coverage for your child's instrument (subject, of course, to your deductible).
- Take your child's instrument in for a checkup twice a year.
- Supervise your child to make sure he takes care of his instrument properly.
- Don't attempt repair of your child's instrument — leave it to an expert.
- Seek the recommendation of your child's teacher for a repair technician.
- Band repair technicians belong to NAPBIRT; violin makers belong to AFVBM.

5.

MAKING A SOUND: FIRST NOTES

Every day, music teachers help youngsters deal with those first frustrations that accompany trying to get uncooperative body parts — fingers, hands, arms, mouth — to all work together to produce a sound that won't scare farm animals in the next county! Your child's teacher has probably guided many children through those halting first steps all the way to a successful, rewarding school band or orchestra experience.

In this chapter, I would like to give you a few tips and hints so you can better understand what your child is going through, and so you can help supervise what happens at home.

VISITING THE CLASSROOM

I hope you will visit your child's band or orchestra class for one of the first sessions. Some teachers make it a point to invite parents, in the beginning stages, to accomplish some of the things we will discuss in this chapter.

Keep in mind, however, that a school visit may be impractical or impossible due to space limitations or other restrictions. I've taught in schools where band and strings were held in what amounts to a large closet. There was barely enough room for the students and me, let alone visiting parents! Also, too many visitors in the classroom can diminish the quality of teaching. Children tend to focus more on visitors than they do the teacher, and the

Make it a point to visit your child's band or orchestra class early on.

whole thing begins to resemble a three ring circus.

You should, however, be able to attend at least one of your child's first band or orchestra classes to get a feel for what your child's experience is like so you can help at home.

ASSEMBLING THE INSTRUMENT

Your music dealer or your child's teacher has, I hope, shown you and your child how to assemble the instrument. Practice assembling and disassembling the instrument with your child.

Some instruments, such as the clarinet, have several parts that must be put together carefully and completely. Some youngsters don't have the strength to get clarinet joints tight. If you know how to assemble the instrument, you can help your child and avoid having a joint fall off or break off — initiating an expensive and unnecessary repair.

HOLDING THE INSTRUMENT PROPERLY

Instruments for beginners are, for the most part, very durable. Years of experience have taught major manufacturers how to produce instruments that can withstand most of the abuse (however unintentional) that children visit upon them. No instrument, though, no matter how well constructed, is designed to be twirled, kicked, thrown, dropped off a building, or used as a pull-toy for the family German shepherd.

To avoid the chance of accidental damage, the instrument must be held properly and handled with care. If you don't know the proper way to hold the instrument, you can't correct your child when he forgets.

Your child's method book may show how to hold the instrument when playing it. If not, ask the teacher or music dealer to show you. As with assembling the instrument, practice holding it properly, so you can supervise your child.

Don't be afraid your child's teacher will think you are a pest for asking questions. Most teachers will be delighted to know that

Your child's first performance for you will probably be a "one-note" symphony.

you care enough about your child's success to want to supervise home practice.

FINALLY — PLAYING NOTES

One of the most exciting moments in a child's band and orchestra experience is when he learns to play those first few notes. When this happens, your child will want to run home, tear open the case, and serenade you with that first tune.

Don't expect too much. That first "musical performance" will probably consist of playing a note and holding it out to the count of four; resting for four counts; then playing the note again!

This "one note" symphony will be repeated on each new pitch your child learns. While it isn't exactly a musical opus of monumental proportions, it's a big deal for your child.

Listen, smile, be encouraging, even offer polite applause. (Whistling, stomping your feet, and screaming "Encore!" are not necessary.)

The teacher will show your child how to produce a tone and play notes. It's almost impossible to learn tone production on a musical instrument without "hands-on" experience, so I can't really tell you how to play your child's instrument.

That doesn't mean you can't supervise your child at home. Take a look at your child's beginning method book. Remember, this book was designed for someone who knows nothing about music.

The first few pages probably have letters under the notes as they are introduced. Those are the names of the notes. All music signs and symbols are defined. All you have to do is read.

Ask your child to tell you the name of each note before he plays it. This is called "Say it and Play it" and is a common way children are taught to read music.

The important thing for you to do is to be there when your child practices those first few times. Don't send him off to his room and assume that all will go well. Children need supervision. By being there, even if you can't add to your child's knowledge, you are supervising. Chapter 6 contains more hints on supervising home practice.

EVALUATION OF PROGRESS

It is important for you to understand how your child is doing. At some point you are going to have to decide whether to buy the instrument you have been renting, and a clear evaluation of your child's progress is essential.

Your child's teacher will probably send home one or more written evaluations of the child's progress in band or orchestra. The sorts of things teachers usually comment on include the following:

Attendance

You would be amazed at how many children just stop coming to band or orchestra class, and the parents don't find out about it until there's a program! Band and orchestra teachers usually don't have the time to call the parents every time a child doesn't show. A progress report that comments on attendance will tell you whether your child has been attending regularly.

Home Practice

Some teachers have parents sign a practice chart on a weekly basis, and send it home at the end of the term with comments, so the parent knows if his child needs to put in more practice time. Other teachers simply ask the child how often he practices.

I like to have students keep a monthly record of home practice, which parents sign and send in at the end of each month. I have included one in Appendix B, which you can photocopy and use, if your child's teacher doesn't send one home.

By the way, fifteen to twenty minutes a day of supervised practice is enough to start off.

Participation

If your child attends class but doesn't try, this could be a sign of frustration. If the teacher indicates this is happening with your child, you and the child need to discuss it. You may also want to discuss your concern with the teacher.

Behavior

Misbehavior or "acting up" is sometimes a sign of frustration. This frustration can come as a result of your child's lack of interest, a boring teacher, or lack of progress due to lack of home practice. If poor behavior continues, talk with the teacher.

Progress

Progress has to do with how well and how fast your child is learning notes, producing good tone, and counting rhythms. The teacher's evaluation of progress will indicate whether the child is keeping up with other children in class or falling behind.

You don't want your child to get so far behind that he can't catch up. If overall progress is poor, make an appointment to talk with the teacher to get suggestions on how you can help your child. Also talk with your child to find out if his interest is falling off or if there is some other problem.

RECAP

- Ask for help in learning how to assemble and hold your child's instrument properly. It isn't enough for your child to know these things — you should know them too.
- Visit your child's band or orchestra class early on. You need to get a feel for what your child faces each time he goes to band or orchestra. This way you will be able to help.
- Even though you may not be able to play the instrument, you can supervise your child by sitting down with him and asking him to tell you what he is doing.
- Be sure you understand the teacher's evaluation of your child's progress. If there's something you don't agree with or if you don't understand something, talk to the teacher.
- Keep a record of your child's home practice. Fifteen to twenty minutes a day is enough.

The next chapter will help you get your child through the difficult times. It's one of the most important chapters in the book, because it will be your involvement here that might spell the difference between success and failure for your child.

6.

KEEPING UP INTEREST

Nationally, almost half the children who start on a band or orchestra instrument drop out within the first year. Many reasons are given, but for those of us who believe any child can be taught to play an instrument, there is really only one reason: *The child lost interest.*

Children often lose interest because the teacher talks too much or is boring, or because the teacher and parents don't provide the support needed to get the child through the inevitable rough times that follow the beginning stages of learning to play an instrument.

You can do more to keep your child from dropping out of band or orchestra than anyone else, including the teacher. If the band or orchestra teacher is boring, you can put excitement into your child's musical life.

HELPING YOUR CHILD PRACTICE

Nobody likes to practice. Your child doesn't — if you played an instrument in school, you didn't — and I didn't. To this day, the sound of a child playing scales on a piano sends chills down my spine. When I was a kid, I would rather have had my teeth cleaned with a belt sander than practice piano!

You can help your child practice, even if you don't know how to read music. Supervision is the key. If you make sure your child follows a system like the one outlined below, you will be doing a lot to increase the efficiency of his practice time. And the more efficient his practice time, the less time he will have to spend practicing!

How Often?

Your child should practice every day, preferably at the same time each day. A regular practice time is best because it's easier to get a child to follow a routine, once it is established, than it is to practice "hit or miss."

If your child does miss a day — and no child can be expected to practice consistently seven days a week — don't try to make up the time. The important thing is: Try to set a regular time each day and stick with it.

How Long?

The idea that it takes hours and hours of daily practice to learn how to play an instrument probably comes from band and orchestra teachers who love to tell their students about how when they were in college, they used to practice "until their lips and fingers bled"!

I'll tell you a little secret. In four years of undergraduate school, I never once saw a music major shed blood in the practice room. I did see a trombone player get roughed up once, but it wasn't from practicing. He made a wrong turn during a marching band halftime show and got run over by the tuba section. It wasn't a pretty sight.

The point is, an hour a day is too much for most beginners to practice an instrument. They simply don't have the endurance for it. Fifteen to twenty minutes a day is much more realistic.

Besides, the biggest problem teachers have with beginners is not that they don't practice enough. It's that they don't practice *right*.

Children waste a lot of practice time going over things they already know. They don't want to learn anything new. Children also spend a lot of practice time sitting without playing. They stare at the book. Then they stare at the instrument. Then they stare at the wall. Then they stare at the book again. In other words, children do the same thing adults do when facing an unpleasant task. They procrastinate!

Reprinted with special permission of North America Syndicate, Inc.

What is needed then, is a practice system or routine that you, the parent, can enforce.

The Practice Session

Beginners should start each practice session with a review of notes already learned. Have your child play his notes for you, naming each one, and holding each note out to the count of four or eight.

Playing long, slow tones is called "warming up." Children don't like to warm up and, as a result, have difficulty developing good tone. By supervising the warmup period and having the child name and play the notes, you will accomplish two things: (1) Your child will learn to warm up properly; and (2) he will begin to learn to read music.

Percussion players, obviously, can't hold notes out, but they can start slow, practicing alternating strokes, and learning note names on the bells.

Children should, from the very beginning, train themselves to look at the *music* when they play — not at their hands. Naturally, they need to check finger position, etc., but the sooner they start keeping their eyes on the music, they sooner they will learn to "read."

The warmup should be from three to five minutes long, depending on how many notes the child has learned. This should be followed by playing through a new exercise in the method book.

For most children, this exercise will be something that has been gone through at school — something that has been assigned for home practice. Few beginners are able to "work ahead," unless the new material is similar to material already learned.

The child should play all the way through, the best he can, without stopping, no matter how many mistakes he makes. Then he should go back and work on the hard parts. This is the part children hate most! They want to play the songs they know and can do well on, and don't want to go through the repetition and drill needed to learn new passages.

Try turning it into a game. Have your child identify a section he is having trouble with — the shorter the section the better — then have him "drill" or practice that section until he can play it correctly at least four times, before going on.

Don't allow your child to bite off more than he can chew. That is, don't let him try to go all the way through an entire exercise when there is really only one small section that needs work.

OK, time out!

What if you are sitting there, trying to supervise your child as he drills on something you can't even read? How will you know when he gets it right once, let alone four times?

Easy. You won't. But it doesn't matter!

The important point is: You are making your child follow a *system* for practicing. Even if your child's band or orchestra teacher were there, supervising practice, chances are the teacher would have to let some things slide.

Even if the child makes mistakes, the repetition will help. And it will be infinitely better than letting your child stare at the wall. Besides, your child is getting help at school and, as time goes on, he will be more and more certain of what he is doing.

As soon as your child has drilled his way through the exercise, he should play it again all the way through. Depending on how much time is spent on the practice session, the child can now go on to another exercise or section of music and repeat the process of playing it all the way through; breaking it down and drilling on the hard parts; then conclude by playing it all the way through again.

Each practice session should end with something familiar that your child can play well. It's important that he finish with a positive feeling about playing his instrument.

PRACTICE AIDS: METRONOMES, TUNERS, AND VIDEOS

A metronome is a device that can be set to click with a steady beat at different speeds to help your child develop rhythm and counting skills. Metronomes come in all shapes, sizes, and prices, but you can get a good one for about $25. Check with your local music dealer or look through one of the mail order music catalogs.

The second item, the electronic tuner, measures the sound your child plays and tells him if he is too high, too low, or just right (in tune). Some tuners even "sample" the pitch and indicate the name of the note, as well as whether it is in tune or not.

As your child grows musically, he must learn to use his "ear" to tell whether he is in tune or not, but all professional musicians use tuners. I have found that beginners can use them — especially the ones that read pitches — to great advantage.

Tuners are not cheap. Even a "no-frills" tuner will cost more than $100 — less from a mail order catalog. Ask your child's teacher for advice before buying a tuner. It's hard to go wrong on a metronome, but tuners are tricky.

String players need to learn how to tune the strings on their instrument. This can be done using an electronic tuner, a tuning fork, a pitch pipe, or a piano. Since improper tuning of stringed instruments can cause damage to the instrument, however, I don't recommend buying any sort of tuner for a string player without first consulting the orchestra teacher.

Finally, a company called Music Education Video offers a series of sixty minute lessons for beginners on band instruments. These videotapes provide reinforcement during that critical first three months of study and only cost about $25 each. See Appendix D for the address and phone number.

PRIVATE LESSONS

Letting your child have private lessons is a great way to encourage him and help him make progress learning to play his instrument. A good private teacher will challenge your child to be the very best musician he can be and, at the same time, provide support and help when your child needs it most. No matter how dedicated your child's band or orchestra teacher is, he will not be able to give your child the individual attention a private teacher can.

Private lessons are not the same as tutoring in other school

One of the best ways to encourage your child and keep up interest is with private lessons.

subjects. In other words, private lessons are not "remedial." Children don't take private lessons in order to catch up with other children. Private lessons enable a student to get ahead and stay ahead. Private lessons take place at a music store, at the home of the private teacher, at school, or even in your home.

A typical private lesson is thirty minutes long. Most private teachers, though, are poor "clock watchers" and lessons often run thirty-five or forty minutes. Unless, of course, the teacher has students scheduled back to back.

Cost depends on the area and the professional level of the private teacher, but $10 per weekly half-hour lesson is about average. Each teacher has his own policy regarding payment in advance, making up missed lessons, etc. In general, you will probably have to pay for the lesson if you don't give at least twenty-four hours notice before cancelling or rescheduling. Some teachers want to be paid a month in advance and don't give refunds, they just reschedule the missed lesson.

Your child's band or orchestra teacher can help in choosing a private teacher and will know which ones work best with children.

EMOTIONAL HIGHS AND LOWS

Your child will experience many emotional highs and lows as he learns to play his instrument. Some days he will come home from band, orchestra, or his private lesson and can't wait to show you what he has learned. On other days, he will be so sullen you will think music is a military secret!

Learn to go with the flow. Ask how class or the lesson went, but don't push it if occasionally, he doesn't want to talk about it. He may have had a bad day and doesn't want to relive it. If it gets to the point where your child never wants to talk about band or orchestra, then it's time to talk with the teacher.

Sometimes, students quit coming to class and don't tell their parents until just before a concert. Most band and orchestra teachers see many children each week, and they don't always talk with parents often enough to realize when there is a problem. You see your child every day. Make it a point to ask about band or orchestra and get in touch with the teacher if a problem develops.

Every young musician experiences emotional highs and lows.
Photo by Tim Sams.

ENCOURAGEMENT AND PRAISE

It is important that you encourage your child in learning to play his instrument. Sometimes this is hard to do when the sounds you hear coming out of the bedroom make you wonder if he is torturing some small animal instead of practicing!

Try to say something positive about your child's progress every day. It doesn't have to be much, just something to let him know you are paying attention and you care. If your child is struggling and doesn't seem to be making progress, stop him for a while. Maybe he needs a break from the instrument for a day or two. We all go through days when we can't seem to do anything right.

OTHER REWARDS

Encouragement and praise from you and the teacher are the best rewards a beginner gets. Nothing means more than a kind word, a smile, a pat on the back. Children don't always show it, but they thrive on our praise. From time to time, however, more tangible rewards are in order.

I don't recommend you overdo this. After all, music should be its own reward. If we start giving out "prizes" for learning to play an instrument, we might encourage the wrong kind of attitude. The next thing you know, your child will be featured soloist with the Los Angeles Philharmonic, and it will cost you $25 just to hear him play! And all because I suggested you get him a milk shake and a Big Mac for learning "Go Tell Aunt Rhodie"!

One of our goals is for the child to practice every day. You might consider a special treat or privilege at the end of the month if your child manages to practice every day that month.

Records and tapes are available that you can buy for your child to play along with. These can be used as rewards and are good motivators as well. The most well known play-along series is called "Music Minus One®."

The Music Minus One® series includes records and tapes in all musical formats. Everything from classical to rock is represented. Most large music stores have play-along records and tapes or they can order them for you.

Many play-along records and cassettes are more appropriate for junior high and high school level musicians than beginners. Some beginner method books, though, feature play-along cassette tapes. You can get one of these play-along methods as supplemental material to use at home, even if your child uses another book at school.

Most play-along methods cost less than $10. Check at your local music store or in one of the mail order catalogs.

Appendix D lists a couple of companies that market music-related gifts. Consider an unusual musical gift as a reward for your child. You can also use these catalogs to buy something special for birthdays, Christmas, or other special occasions.

OTHER WAYS TO KEEP UP INTEREST

A variety of other ways exist to enhance your child's enjoyment as he learns to play a band or orchestra instrument.

Attending Concerts and Recitals

Your child should see and hear live performances of high school, college, and professional groups as well as individuals who play his instrument.

Professional Musical Groups

Unless you live at the North Pole, you are probably closer to a professional symphony orchestra than you think. There are more than 160 major, regional, and metropolitan orchestras in the United States. If you add community orchestras, there are many, many more. Look in your telephone book or the telephone book of the nearest large city for the name of a professional or community symphony orchestra near you. Call and ask to be sent subscription or ticket information.

Many symphony orchestras schedule lighter concerts for less experienced concertgoers. Quite a few even have concerts tailored to children.

Attending a professional symphony concert is not cheap. You can expect to pay $10 or more for a ticket. It's good to know, in advance, whether the music that has been programmed is something your child might enjoy.

There are very few professional concert bands anymore, but they do exist. Find out if there's a professional band in your city and, if so, plan to attend one of their concerts. Outdoor band concerts are always entertaining and fun.

All five of the Armed Forces have professional music groups, and most are based in Washington, DC. If you visit Washington, plan to attend one of the free service band concerts on the lawn of the White House.

The top service bands also tour all over the country. If you have the opportunity to hear one of them in concert, by all means, take advantage. Most concerts by the service bands are free or there is a nominal charge to cover the cost of the performance hall.

If there is a military installation near you and it has a band, chances are the band performs concerts on and off base. Call the base and ask about performances that are open to the public.

Community and College Groups

If you live in or near a city with a college or university that has a music department, call the music department and ask to be sent a calendar of musical events. Most colleges will be only too happy to oblige, and you will have a wealth of live performances to choose from — all the way from visiting professional symphony orchestras to solo recitals by music majors. The best part is that most of these performances are free or nominal in cost.

If you aren't sure what type of music you will hear at a specific concert, call the music department and ask. University concerts are geared more to college music majors than they are to beginners.

Many cities have a community orchestra or band. These groups are made up of volunteer musicians and perform many times throughout the year. As with most college groups, community band and orchestra concerts are usually free.

Churches

Local churches are another source of live performances. Most newspapers run a section, at least once a week, in which area church services and special events are listed. Many of these special events are purely musical events — not religious services. Most church performances are free or involve a "free will" offering.

Make sure your child hears groups that he may join someday.

Junior and Senior High School Groups

Your child should hear the local high school and junior high groups that he will, one day, be part of. Annual "events" calendars often list all the concerts and musical events that will occur during the coming school year. Sometimes the school band or orchestra teacher sends home notices of these events and encourages beginners to attend. If not, call the junior high or high school office and get the dates of music department concerts.

Listening to (and Viewing) Records and Tapes

Your child should hear his instrument played by professionals in order to learn good tone. One of the best ways to accomplish this is to check out records and cassette tapes from your local public library. Look under the Instrumental Music category for recordings of professionals playing your child's instrument.

Also, check out orchestra and band recordings so your child will begin to hear what constitutes good ensemble (group) sound.

Listening to music should not be merely background music when doing homework. Your child needs to be able to concentrate on the music and learn from what he hears.

On the other hand, don't make your child sit quietly and listen for hours on end, either. One or two cuts from a record are really enough — unless, of course, your child really wants to hear more.

Many public libraries also have videotapes for loan. Some of them are of musicals, operas, and so forth. These tapes don't usually feature instrumental musicians. Shorter videos that feature bands, orchestras, and instrumental groups are available, however, and can be checked out free just like records and cassette tapes.

If your child plays one of the brass instruments, look for any of the videotapes made by the Canadian Brass. The Canadian Brass tapes are funny, entertaining, and informative. The music is excellent and well played. Many schools use Canadian Brass videotapes as recruiting tools for the band program.

Playing for Family and Friends

In addition to hearing other groups and individuals, your child will benefit from the opportunity to perform for others. As soon as he gains some ability, allow him to volunteer to play for church, family, and friends.

Don't become a "stage parent" — someone who stands in the wings and pushes his child to perform and be in the limelight all the time, but do encourage your child to perform for others.

Try to make it a pleasant experience. Don't encourage your child to play when he isn't ready — and don't ever *make* him perform in public. Children vary widely in the amount of enthusiasm they have for performing in front of other people. This should be allowed to develop as naturally as possible.

Make a Tape (Video or Audio)

If you have a cassette recorder, tape your child and play it back for him to hear. He can learn a lot by listening to and criticizing his own playing. You can do the same with a video camera. Your child can benefit from seeing himself to help correct posture problems.

If you videotape family activities, don't forget to get some footage of your child practicing his instrument. A few years from now you can drag out that tape and remember why you had the basement soundproofed!

Computer Programs and Games

If you have a computer, especially an IBM, an Apple, or a Commodore, there are a number of computer programs available to help reinforce music learning. There are programs that teach note reading, rhythms, music terms and, with some special hardware, even fingerings. These computer programs are often entertaining and, considering the affinity children have for video games, might be well worth considering. Not counting the programs that require special hardware, most sell for around $50 and are designed to be used by beginners as well as college students.

Several mail order catalogs list computer programs, or you can ask at school for recommendations of specific programs that your child's teacher uses and likes.

Most regular computer software dealers don't sell specialized music software, but some music dealers are beginning to, especially those that are getting into "midi" instruments and other forms of computerized music.

RECAP

- You can help your child practice, even if you don't know how to read music.
- Your child should practice every day for fifteen to twenty minutes.
- Practice should begin with warmup, followed by a systematic drill on new material, and conclude with something the child knows and plays well.
- Practice aids (metronome, tuner, videotape lessons) can enhance your child's lessons.
- Private lessons are one of the best ways I know of to encourage your child and help him progress on his instrument.
- Your child will experience many emotional highs and lows as he learns to play his instrument.
- It is very important that you encourage and praise your child frequently.
- Occasionally give other rewards, such as a trip to a fast food restaurant or a small gift.
- Take your child to concerts and recitals, both as a reward and as a way to let him hear fine music.
- Make sure your child listens to records of accomplished artists playing his instrument. You can buy recordings or borrow them from the library.
- Encourage your child to play for family and friends.
- Include your child playing his instrument in family videos.
- If you have a computer, there are entertaining programs available that provide drill and reinforcement of music learning.

We have discussed many ways you, as a parent, can provide encouragement and support for your child. The most important element you bring to your child's musical experience, however, is *you*.

By helping to supervise home practice and by attending concerts and listening to records together, you are sending a very powerful message to your child. You are saying that your child's success is very important to you and that you are willing to invest time and energy to make sure he has a chance to succeed.

7.

UPGRADING TO A BETTER INSTRUMENT

I know what you are thinking. You just started renting an instrument, and already I'm talking about upgrading to something better. Actually, this chapter is for later.

At some point the subject of upgrading to a better quality or professional model instrument will come up. The purpose of this chapter is to help you know when the time to upgrade has arrived, and to help you make the right decisions when it does.

WHEN TO UPGRADE

There is no magic age when your child should upgrade to a higher quality instrument. It's a matter of musical maturity — something that varies from individual to individual.

Most students who upgrade, though, do so as they go into high school. That's not etched in stone, of course. And just because your child is "musically" ready for a better instrument, doesn't mean you have to get one.

A lot of factors come into play: Your child's long-term music goals, for example. Does he plan to continue playing in college? Is he a serious musician or simply someone who has fun with it? And finally, it depends on the advice of your child's private teacher.

PRIVATE LESSONS FIRST, UPGRADE SECOND

Learning to play an instrument is a skill. This skill must be taught. It doesn't matter how much you pay for a professional quality instrument for your child; without good private instruction, he will probably not realize his full potential.

There's no value in owning a Mercedes Benz if you don't know how to drive. Your child will only benefit from a professional instrument if he has the technique to produce a "professional" sound.

Some will argue that a professional quality instrument is a better instrument and that your child will automatically produce a better tone on it. Maybe so, but I don't think the difference in sound is worth the hundreds—perhaps thousands—of dollars you will have to pay for it. Private lessons come first; instrument upgrade, second.

There are so many different models and quality levels of band and orchestra instruments, that I'm certain no one has ever made a list of them. And even if someone wanted to, I doubt he could find enough paper to do the job without leveling the Amazon rain forest.

Since I don't want to see South America end up a parking lot, I have listed below some generally accepted terms that describe various price and quality levels of instruments for purposes of our discussion in this book.

ORCHESTRA INSTRUMENTS

As a beginning string player, your child will probably start on a down-size student line instrument. You will rent this instrument until your child is large enough for full-size.

When it's time to buy, you will have a choice of buying a student line instrument or one of better quality. Many string players, when they go to full-size, buy an instrument that's a step or two above student line.

New Instruments

Most new stringed instruments are made in West Germany, Hungary, or Japan and sold under various names by distributors in the United States.

Differences in price and quality for new stringed instruments have to do with the quality of the materials used, the amount of handcrafting that goes into the making of the instrument, and the amount of shop adjusting that is done before the instrument is sold.

New stringed instruments range in price from a little under $500 up to several thousand dollars. The very best professional quality new instruments are said to rival some of the most well-known "old" instruments.

"Old" Instruments

Serious string players don't buy new, they buy "old." That is, they buy "previously-owned, proven" instruments that appreciate in value the older they get.

These are not student line instruments, but ones that are principally handcrafted.

You've probably heard of the most famous "old" stringed instruments — those made by Antonio Stradivari in the 1700s. These instruments are considered to be the finest in the world and when sold at auction, go for up to a million dollars apiece.

There are, however, many other "old" instruments — not as old as a Stradivarius — that are bought by serious students in high school and college.

What Do Most Students Get When They Upgrade?

Most string students buy a new instrument of a little better quality than student line. For a violin, they typically pay between $600 and $800.

Some serious students upgrade again before going to college and buy an "old" instrument for anywhere from $3000 to $5000 or more.

Where to Shop

Violin shops and violin "brokers" (specialists in "old" instruments) are the primary sources for upgrading a stringed instrument. Private teachers also often know of available instruments, and *Strings* magazine (Appendix E) lists a variety of sources for better quality instruments.

The principal source for a professional string upgrade is a violin shop or a violin "broker."

Your child will probably have to try several different instruments from several different sources before finding one that's right. It is not unusual for a serious student to search for several years before finding an instrument he or she likes.

Have the private teacher or orchestra director look any instrument over before you buy it.

BAND INSTRUMENTS

There are basically three different grades of band instruments: student line, step-up or intermediate, and professional. Classification, as with stringed instruments, depends on the quality of the materials used, the amount of handcrafting involved, and the degree to which the instruments are hand-adjusted before being sold.

Student Line

The student line model is the one most beginners start on. These instruments are made to be as musical as possible, while still maintaining durability. Many students play a student line instrument all the way through high school.

A typical regular student line band instrument lists for about $450. Naturally, special instruments, such as saxophone, French horn, oboe, and bassoon, cost more.

Step-up

Costing a few hundred dollars more than a student line instrument, step-up models have features that the low-end instruments don't offer.

In general, I don't feel most step-up models are worth the extra cost. I think you would be better off to save your money and buy a top of the line instrument later.

A few step-up models, however, are really semi-pro instruments and might be worth considering. Your child's private teacher or band teacher can guide you if you are considering buying a step-up model.

Professional Model

These are the top of the line instruments — supposedly the ones the professional musicians play. This is what you get when you are really serious about music. Prices vary, but a typical new, professional model band instrument can run anywhere from $1000 and up.

What Do Most Students Get When They Upgrade?

Most band students who upgrade go with a professional model — typically during high school. Sometimes they buy a used professional instrument rather than a new one and pay about half the price of a new professional model.

Options

Just as with automobiles, professional band instruments offer a variety of options. These include such performance-oriented items as a "low B foot" on flute or extra keys or tuning slides on other instruments. They also include "cosmetic" options such as a special finish.

Not all "performance" options are necessary or desirable for every student. Your child's private teacher will guide you when it comes to choosing the right options for your child.

Where to Shop

Your local music dealer handles professional model band instruments, but unless the store is quite large, he may not have a quantity of them in stock for your child to try. Often, the local dealer can get several different models in "on approval." You will probably have to ask him to do this.

Mail order dealers generally have a larger selection, but that does you no good unless your child can actually try them out. Some mail order dealers have retail outlets and if you live close enough, it might be worth the drive.

Private teachers are a good source for professional model instruments. An advanced student may be getting a new instrument and have a used professional or semi-pro model for sale.

You might also contact a local independent repair technician. Sometimes repair technicians obtain high quality instruments at "bargain-basement" prices, fix them up, and sell them for much less than you would pay at a music store.

It's best if your child can try several different instruments before deciding. As always, have the private teacher or band director look the instrument over before buying it.

KEEPING THE OLD INSTRUMENT

You may want to keep your child's student line instrument instead of selling it or trading it in. This way your child will have a marching band or pep band instrument or (in the case of a stringed instrument) an instrument to hand down to a younger brother or sister when he or she is old enough to join band or orchestra.

SELLING THE OLD INSTRUMENT

If you own a student line instrument and want to sell it after upgrading, sell it yourself. Trading it in is a waste of time and effort.

Most music dealers already have more used instruments than they can sell.

Put an ad in the paper or tell your child's music teacher you have an instrument for sale. Set a fair price. Your child's teacher can help. Typically, a used student line instrument will sell for anywhere from $100 to $200.

Remember, most beginners rent at first, then end up buying the instrument they rent. If you have a used instrument for sale, your price has to be so attractive that someone who has rented for several months will come out ahead by buying your instrument and giving up the rent which would have applied to purchase.

WARRANTY, INSURANCE, MAINTENANCE, AND REPAIR

New professional model instruments purchased from a music dealer carry warranties just like student line instruments. (Review the information in Chapter 4.)

There are differences, though. For example, a professional model clarinet is made of wood — which may only carry a six-month warranty against cracking — as opposed to a plastic student line clarinet which has a five-year guarantee against breaking.

Since professional model instruments are not rented, damage and theft insurance isn't offered by the music dealer. Your instrument is probably covered for theft by your homeowner's policy (subject, of course, to a deductible), and there are companies that sell musical instrument insurance (see Appendix E). Except for manufacturing defects and store warranties, maintenance and repair of your professional instrument are your responsibility.

The higher the quality level of the instrument, the more specialized the repair. Professional violinists, for example, have been known to fly their expensive instruments to New York (first class, no less) for repair and maintenance. You should rely on your child's private teacher for recommendations regarding repair of professional quality instruments.

As with student line instruments, don't attempt any repair yourself. There are no "user adjustable" parts on a professional instrument. Most professional musicians don't attempt to repair their instrument themselves, so why should you?

When upgrading, make sure your child tries several different instruments before choosing. Photo by Tim Sams.

RECAP

- Most students upgrade as they go into high school, though it's really a matter of musical maturity.
- Do not upgrade your child's instrument unless he is studying privately.
- Quality (and price) of musical instruments depends on material used, amount of hand crafting, and amount of shop adjusting.
- Top level instruments can be bought new or used ("old," in the case of strings).
- Your child's private teacher will advise you on which options to consider.
- Most students should keep their old instrument to use for marching band, pep band, or a younger brother or sister.
- If you decide to sell, sell it outright — do not try to sell to a music dealer or trade it in.
- New and used instrument warranties are provided for step-up instruments in much the same way as they are for student line models.

- Insurance is generally your responsibility.
- Once you get beyond the initial warranty, maintenance and repair are your responsibility.
- Do not attempt any repair of a professional quality instrument.

Upgrading to a better quality instrument is not a necessity. Many children go through school playing the same instrument they started on. If you decide, however, to invest in a professional level instrument, shop around and make sure your child tries several instruments before making a choice.

In the next chapter we will discuss enhancing your child's music experience by participating in other musical groups.

8.
PERFORMANCE OPPORTUNITIES

As your child gets older he will have more and more opportunities to use the skills learned as an instrumental musician. At first, there's Band Class or String Class. But as the years go on, the opportunities grow. Band and orchestra are still the main groups, of course, but as your child moves into the higher grades, he has many other musical options.

In this chapter we'll take a brief look at some of the other musical performance opportunities your child will have during his school years and beyond.

ELEMENTARY SCHOOL

As a beginner, your child will be in a class with other beginners on band or orchestra instruments. The beginning band or orchestra will probably perform at school one or two times during the school year.

Private Lesson Recitals

Additional performance opportunities may come through private lessons. Many private teachers have recitals featuring their students. Private teacher recitals help children learn to perform in public and offer a receptive forum for creative self-expression.

Community Summer Programs

Some communities have summer bands or orchestras for beginners. Ask your child's band or orchestra teacher also about privately sponsored summer programs that offer performance opportunities for youngsters with only a moderate amount of experience.

Church and Scout Groups

Beginners are sometimes asked to play in church and at various other functions, such as Boy Scouts, Girl Scouts, etc. Most children aren't ready for this kind of public exposure until they have studied for a couple of years. Don't put pressure on your elementary child to perform publicly. Public performance should be a natural outgrowth of learning to play an instrument, not a stress-filled obstacle.

MIDDLE/JUNIOR HIGH SCHOOL

Your child's middle school or junior high band or orchestra will perform several times during the school year. Most schools have a holiday program before Christmas vacation and at least one more in the spring.

For many students, middle school or junior high is their first encounter with music competition. There are two basic types of music competition for band and orchestra students. Both types are usually sponsored by the state music educators' association.

Solo/Ensemble Contest

In Solo/Ensemble Contest, students perform solos or in small groups called "ensembles." Students are rated by an adjudicator — a high school or university teacher who specializes on the instrument or instruments he judges. After performing, students receive a "rating" — I, II, III, etc. and a "comment sheet."

The comment sheet contains an evaluation and includes positive comments as well as suggestions for improvement. The rating lets the student know how he performed against a "standard of excellence."

Some band and orchestra teachers prefer all students to go to contest; others leave it up to the student. Many private teachers encourage students to go to contest and spend part of every lesson helping them prepare a solo or ensemble.

A fee is charged for each student who participates in Solo Contest. This fee is paid by the student. If your child participates in Solo Contest, he will probably also need to have someone accompany him on piano. The accompanist can be a high school student, a family friend, a church organist, or a teacher.

Large Group Contest

Large Group Contest is for the whole band or orchestra and usually occurs near the end of the year. As with Solo/Ensemble Contest, some teachers are big on it, others are not.

In Large Group Contest, a panel of music judges evaluates the group's performance of several musical selections and offers written and taped comments and a rating, as in Solo/Ensemble Contest.

The purpose of Large Group Contest (like Solo/Ensemble Contest) is to provide students an opportunity to be evaluated and to learn from that evaluation.

Community Summer Programs

By junior high school age, there is a variety of summer programs available to young musicians. Check with your child's teacher for information on local music programs, which are often sponsored by the city recreation department.

Summer Music Camps

Instrumentalist magazine (Appendix E) publishes an annual national list of summer music camps. Some of these camps have programs for junior high students. Your child's band or orchestra teacher may know of camps in your area, including live-in or day camps at local universities and colleges.

HIGH SCHOOL

High school is where the fun really begins! By the time your child gets into the high school music program, he will have a number of musical activities to choose from. His main musical outlet, of course, will still be either Concert Band or Orchestra.

Like their middle school/junior high counterparts, high school performance groups give several concerts annually and often participate in the high school versions of Solo/Ensemble Contest and Large Group Contest.

Marching Band

The main fall musical activity, in most high schools, is marching band. Marching band usually starts with "band camp" in August before school begins. Band camp is about a week long and can be at school or away. If your child goes away for band camp, expect to pay about $100 for room and board for the week.

Marching bands perform in parades, at football games, at festivals, and at contests. On any fall weekend, hundreds of marching band festivals and contests are held all across the country. In fact, in some areas you see more school buses on Saturday morning than you do during the rest of the week!

The main fall musical activity in most high schools is marching band.

Strolling Strings (Orchestra)

The orchestra doesn't march, but sometimes it strolls! Strolling strings perform mostly memorized light pop music for banquets and similar functions and literally "stroll" or move around from table to table, stopping occasionally to perform, then moving on.

Strolling string groups, patterned after the Air Force Strolling Strings at the White House, have become popular in high school orchestras and provide the orchestra teacher with an answer to the band's "jazz ensemble."

Full Orchestra (Orchestra and Selected Band)

In high school, orchestra usually includes the first chair or top players from the band and is called "full" orchestra. If your child is one of the top band musicians, he will probably be invited to participate in orchestra. All string players are automatically in full orchestra.

Musical (Orchestra and Selected Band)

Participating in orchestra may also include performing in an annual musical or operetta. Playing in a musical orchestra involves many evening rehearsals and lots of hard work. Somehow, though, it all seems worth it on opening night.

Since the musical "pit" orchestra is usually smaller than the full orchestra, it is sometimes necessary for students to audition to be in those groups.

Pep Band

During winter, many schools have a pep band that plays marching band music at basketball games. The basketball pep band usually sits in the stands, often with a student director (supervised by a music teacher) and sometimes includes some electric instruments such as guitar, electric bass, synthesizer, etc.

Jazz Ensemble (Band)

Many high school band programs today have a jazz ensemble — a group that includes saxophones, trumpets, trombones, piano, guitar, electric bass, and drum set. In some schools, the jazz ensemble takes the place of the basketball pep band and performs at home basketball games.

Though the jazz ensemble is really part of the band program, some orchestra musicians learn to play electric or bass guitar or piano, and are able to be a part of this group.

Honors Groups (Selected Orchestra and Band)

State music teacher associations, colleges and universities, and local symphony orchestras often sponsor special "honors" groups for high school band and orchestra musicians.

Typically, these organizations meet over a weekend or a couple of days, rehearse with a special guest conductor, and perform a concert, either for a music convention or as part of a special celebration on campus or in the community.

Honors bands and orchestras are usually open by tryout only, and with the recommendation of the school music teacher.

Youth Orchestras

If your community has a professional symphony orchestra, they might sponsor a youth orchestra. Youth orchestras are select groups — normally open by audition only. Youth orchestras are an excellent way for talented string, wind, and percussion players to be challenged and to grow musically.

Community Summer Programs

Many outside-of-school music groups for high school age students exist. Depending on your area the list might include: community musical theater, a university-sponsored band or orchestra, city recreation department groups or programs, and even a band or orchestra sponsored by a local corporation.

Summer Music Camps

Don't forget the list of summer music camps, published each spring, in the *Instrumentalist*. Your child's teacher will be familiar with many of these national camps and will be able to recommend a good camp for your child.

Don't overlook the possibility of a local summer music camp.

Your child will have many summer performance opportunities in high school.

Some communities have excellent programs that are held as day camps at a local high school or college.

AFTER HIGH SCHOOL

In college your child will have many musical opportunities — marching band, concert band, orchestra, jazz ensemble, etc. Most colleges and universities have instrumental performance groups for all students — those who choose to major in music and those who don't. Many communities have a community orchestra or adult concert band, made up of volunteer musicians from all walks of life.

A FINAL NOTE

Every summer I work with a 120-member high school concert band sponsored by the NCR Corporation. The NCR Concert Band performs weekly concerts at NCR's Old River Park and has been in existence forty-five years.

The NCR Band was started by Dayton music educator Clark Haines in 1945. One of the reasons was that there were very few musical opportunities for young people outside of their high school band or orchestra. Today, as you can tell from the brief descriptions listed in this chapter, there are many.

As I said in Chapter 1, learning to play an instrument is an investment that lasts a lifetime!

Reprinted with special permission of North America Syndicate, Inc.

RECAP

- As your child gets older there will be more and more opportunities to use the skills he has learned as an instrumental musician.
- For beginners there are private lessons, summer recreation programs, church, friends and family.
- Middle school/junior high age youngsters will also add Solo/ Ensemble Contest, Large Group Contest, and some other groups such as marching band, pep band, jazz ensemble.
- High school is where it all happens: marching band, strolling strings, full orchestra, musicals, pep band, jazz ensemble, honors groups.
- There is "musical life" after high school.
- Universities and colleges cater to music majors and non-majors alike when it comes to instrumental performance opportunities.
- Many communities sponsor adult bands and orchestras.

In this chapter we explored a few of the many performance activities your child may have as he goes through his school years and beyond. The next chapter is for parents only. No kids allowed.

9.
YOUR ROLE AS A MUSIC PARENT

This is a catch-all chapter. In it, we will take a brief look at music parents' organizations — sometimes called band parents or orchestra parents — and we will talk about working with the band or orchestra teacher — including how to complain and get results!

MUSIC PARENTS

Most band and orchestra parent groups are found in the high school. The reason is simple: There is no need for parent support groups in elementary, middle, or junior high school. The main activities of high school music parents' groups — fund raising, chaperoning, and uniforms—are not a part of the elementary and middle school experience.

JOIN THE PTA OR PTO

While your child is in elementary and middle school, get involved with the "all-school" parent support groups, such as the PTA or PTO. You can be an advocate for your child and at the same time gain valuable experience before going into combat as a high school music parent!

Believe me, when that day comes, and you chaperone your

Reprinted with special permission of North America Syndicate, Inc.

first "road trip," you will be thankful for every second you spent learning how to dodge spit wads and other flying objects!

PURPOSE AND PHILOSOPHY OF MUSIC PARENTS' GROUPS

The purpose of music parents' groups is to *support* the music program. Plain and simple.

The music program consists of a course of study, developed by the music staff and adopted by the Board of Education. The course of study describes what is taught at various grade levels and adheres to all applicable state and federal laws and regulations.

The band or orchestra teacher must follow the adopted music course of study. He isn't free to change it just because a parent doesn't like something about it.

Most band and orchestra teachers welcome new ideas and suggestions from parents — as long as the parents understand that a "suggestion" is that and nothing more. Parent groups can make suggestions, but cannot dictate curriculum.

FUND RAISING

Fund raising is one of the most important functions of any music parents' group. Most high school band and orchestra programs would shut down if parents quit selling pizzas, holding bake sales, and raffling off trips to Aruba.

Parent groups spend hundreds of hours every year raising money to support school bands and orchestras. Literally thousands of dollars are raised annually for everything from trips and uniforms to semi-trucks and nuclear missiles!

OK, I'm not sure about the nuclear missiles. But I do know of several high school bands that have their own semi-trucks!

TRIPS

Once the pizza sale is over and the money raised to send the band or orchestra to Australia for the "Boomerang Classic," the real work begins: Finding parents crazy enough to go along as chaperones!

After seventeen years of teaching, I have a theory about parents who volunteer to ride on smelly school buses filled with screaming, hyperactive, boom-box-toting teenagers. My theory is this: *These people are nuts!*

I can think of no reason a sane adult would allow himself or herself to be stuffed into a hot, cramped yellow "lunchbox-on-wheels" and spend three and a half hours listening to off-key renditions of "Surfin' U.S.A." with all the words wrong!

Actually, there's really nothing to fear. No parent should ever be afraid to volunteer to chaperone a trip because they don't think they can handle a busload of teenagers. That's silly!

Nobody can! We just fake it, and somehow things always seem to work out for the best. Besides, every trip you go on will include parents who are veterans of previous road trips. You can always spot the veterans. They are the ones in combat fatigues, carrying machetes!

UNIFORMS

Most high school bands and orchestras have some sort of uniform for performances. These uniforms are not purchased by the school. They are paid for by music parents who work very hard raising the thousands of dollars it takes to buy them. A large percentage of the money raised by parent groups goes to pay for and maintain uniforms and accessories.

Most music parents' groups have a standing "uniform committee." The members of the uniform committee fit students at the beginning of the year, maintain and repair the uniforms, and collect them at year's end.

INSTRUMENTS AND EQUIPMENT

High school bands and orchestras need lots of equipment in addition to the things each parent buys for his child. Music has to be provided. Accessories and special props are required for marching band. Sound equipment, risers—the list goes on.

In addition, some instruments are simply too expensive for parents to purchase. In the band, this may include the large background instruments such as percussion, tubas, baritone horns, and French horns. Often included are the more expensive solo instruments such as oboe and bassoon.

Some schools provide all orchestra instruments—violins, violas, cellos, and basses—and rent them out for a nominal fee. In other places, the school owns only the large stringed instruments—cellos and basses. The school board will buy at least some instruments and equipment for the band and orchestra program. Whatever the school board doesn't provide, however, the music parents do!

HELPING WITH PUBLIC RELATIONS

Public relations (PR) is an area where parent organizations can really help. Many parent support groups have a committee or person whose job it is to help "sell" the band or orchestra program to the community.

If you plan to volunteer to help with PR, keep one point in mind: The teacher must review and approve any information that goes out to local media — radio, TV, newspapers, etc. In some school systems, publicity material must undergo further approval through the central office administration. This avoids any problems with a parent unintentionally misrepresenting the school district or the music department. All PR material must go through the teacher in charge. No exceptions.

OTHER WAYS TO HELP

Every music parents' group has a number of committees, all relative to that school music group. These include: Hospitality, Banquets, Sunshine, Decorations, etc.

Find out the names and functions of the various committees and volunteer to be on one or more of them. The best music parents' groups are those in which the greatest number of parents participate.

It isn't enough simply to show up for monthly meetings. The real work of music parents' groups — like most support groups — is done outside of meetings.

RUNNING FOR OFFICE

Most parent associations are governed by a board made up of officers and the music teacher. The board is composed of the elected officers of the association and, sometimes, selected committee chairs.

A complaint sometimes made about parent groups is that the officers or board are "cliquish" — that they don't reflect the makeup of the membership — and that the only way to get on the board is by dying and being "reincarnated" as an officer.

The truth, in most organizations, is that the board is made up of the people who are most active in their child's education from day one. This is why I urge you to become involved in PTA, PTO, and other organizations when your child is in elementary school.

When you become involved in the high school music parents' group, volunteer for at least one committee. Get involved by *doing* something. Show the rest of the group that you care, that you support your child and other children in the band or orchestra.

Officers are usually nominated by a committee that meets in the spring to make nominations for the following year. If you are interested in being an officer for the following year, tell the current President or other members of the board.

Don't be bashful, especially if you really want to be a part of what's going on. The more active your school's music parents' organization, the better the music program will be.

There is a place for you. Don't sit around and wait for someone to call. As they say in the tennis shoe commercial, "Just do it!"

WORKING WITH THE BAND OR ORCHESTRA TEACHER

Chances are your child will have the same band or orchestra teacher for more than one year. Most elementary instrumental teachers also teach in the middle school or junior high, and sometimes even at the high school. It's possible, in fact, that your child will have the same band or orchestra teacher for all his years in school!

This can be both good news and bad news. The good news is that the teacher will get to know your child quite well. The bad news is that the *teacher will get to know your child quite well.*

The problem has to do with expectations. Teachers get used to a child's performance or behavior and tend to expect more of the same. If the expectations are high, it can work to the child's advantage. The teacher will be likely to "cut your child a break" when he occasionally falters. If your child starts off less than brilliantly, however, the teacher may not always recognize improvement.

There may be times, then, when you feel the teacher has been unfair with your child. Solving problems with teachers isn't hard, if you go about it the right way.

HOW TO COMPLAIN

First of all: Talk with the teacher before going to the principal, school board, local newspaper, or Geraldo Rivera.

When you are calm and collected, it's easy to remember that the problem needs to be solved at the source, but when you are upset about something, there is a tendency to want to get action from a higher authority.

In most school districts, you are wasting your time going to an administrator with a teacher problem, unless you have already talked with the teacher and haven't found success. The first question most administrators will ask is: "What did the teacher say when you talked with him?"

Parents whose children are in band or orchestra sometimes feel that if they complain to the teacher, the teacher will take it out on their child. I won't say it doesn't happen. But *most* of the time, if you don't go to the teacher, you won't solve the problem anyway.

Do not discuss an individual problem at a music parents' meeting. You can approach the teacher after the meeting and ask for an appointment, but parent meetings are neither the time nor the place for conferences — unless, of course, the teacher volunteers.

When you *do* talk with the teacher, explain your concern or ask your question as calmly as possible and without accusation. Hysterics are not necessary and are usually counter-productive. They may make you come across as a troublemaker or rabble rouser, not as the concerned parent you really are.

At the conclusion of your conference, don't expect the teacher to suddenly jump up from his chair, embrace you, and shout: "I see your point, Mrs. Smith. You're right. I'm wrong. I'll go kill myself right now!"

A biology teacher, maybe, but not a music teacher.

The fact that you didn't get a signed confession, however, doesn't mean you didn't make your point. Give it a little time and see if things improve. If they do, great!

If not, then go to the building administrator (Principal) and on up through the chain of command. A typical "School System Chain of Command" looks something like this:

Music Teacher
↓
School Principal
↓
Superintendent
↓
School Board

RECAP

- Join the PTA or PTO when your child is in the elementary grades. Get involved now!
- Music parents support the music program — they don't set curriculum.
- One of the most important aspects of "music parents" is raising the money needed to have a quality program.
- High school bands and orchestras go on trips — you are needed to chaperone. (Learn the words to "Surfin' U.S.A.")
- Uniforms for high school music groups are bought by the music parents' group, not the school board.
- Some instruments and equipment are also bought by parent sup-

port groups.
- Parent groups can be a big help with public relations.
- Parent groups have lots of committees — get involved.
- If you want to be an officer, first get on a committee, then tell someone you are interested in running for office. Don't be bashful.
- Your child will have the same band or orchestra teacher for more than one year. This can be good and bad.
- When you have a concern or complaint, go to the teacher first, then the administration. Not vice versa.

This is just about all I have to say about music parents and working with the teacher. And it's almost all I have to say, period.

A few parting words in the Coda and I'm outta here. Thanks for listening. And good luck!

CODA:
THE LAST WORD

The coda is the composer's final chance to say something. Sort of a "musical last word."

That's what this is — *my* last word.

I hope this book has provided some insight into getting your child started on a band or orchestra instrument. After all, that's why I wrote it!

However . . .

THE "NO GUARANTEE" GUARANTEE

Teaching someone to play an instrument is not an exact science. What works for one child may not work for another. Even if your child shows interest and you provide lots of support — including following every bit of advice in this book — there is no way to be certain your child will stick with it and be a happy, successful musician.

All you can do is provide support. That's all anyone can do. However . . .

"TAKE THE OTHER STICK"

When my son was little, I would come home from rehearsal late at night, and find him sitting on his bed, in his pajamas, beside his little toy drum — with his baseball hat on backwards, holding a drum stick and grinning.

"Take the other stick, Daddy," he would say, "Then we can be a BAND!"

Children today seem to "want" so many things — sometimes we forget what they "need."

Children today don't "need" wide-screen TVs, designer tennis shoes, or dolls that perform elective surgery.

Today's children "need" what children have always needed — parents who love them, have patience with them, and support them.

All today's children really need is someone to "take the other stick."

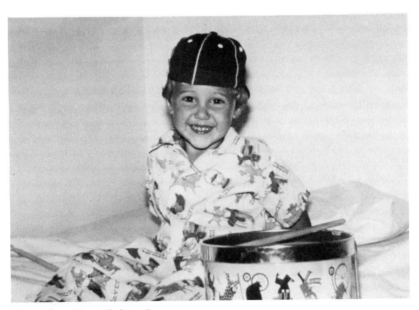

"Take the other stick . . ."

APPENDICES

A: INSTRUMENT PRICE COMPARISON SHEET

Store/Catalog name _____
Phone number _____ Salesman _____
Instrument _____
Brand/Model _____ NEW USED Price $ _____
Guaranteed buy-back? Y N   Within how many months? ____
Price after 3 mos rental? $ _____ After ____ mos? $ _____
Rental/Mo (w/o ins) $ _____   Apply to purchase? Y N
Insurance during rental? Y N   Cost/mo? $ _____
How long can you rent? ____ mos   Financing? Y N
How long? ____ mos APR ____% Monthly pymt $ _____
In-store repair? Y N   Loaners? Y N
NOTES _____
_____

Store/Catalog name _____
Phone number _____ Salesman _____
Instrument _____
Brand/Model _____ NEW USED Price $ _____
Guaranteed buy-back? Y N   Within how many months? ____
Price after 3 mos rental? $ _____ After ____ mos? $ _____
Rental/Mo (w/o ins) $ _____   Apply to purchase? Y N
Insurance during rental? Y N   Cost/mo? $ _____
How long can you rent? ____ mos   Financing? Y N
How long? ____ mos APR ____% Monthly pymt $ _____
In-store repair? Y N   Loaners? Y N
NOTES _____
_____

Store/Catalog name _____
Phone number _____ Salesman _____
Instrument _____
Brand/Model _____ NEW USED Price $ _____
Guaranteed buy-back? Y N   Within how many months? ____
Price after 3 mos rental? $ _____ After ____ mos? $ _____
Rental/Mo (w/o ins) $ _____   Apply to purchase? Y N
Insurance during rental? Y N   Cost/mo? $ _____
How long can you rent? ____ mos   Financing? Y N
How long? ____ mos APR ____% Monthly pymt $ _____
In-store repair? Y N   Loaners? Y N
NOTES _____
_____

B: MONTHLY RECORD OF HOME PRACTICE

Name _____

Month _____

DAY	MIN.	PARENT	DAY	MIN.	PARENT
1			2		
3			4		
5			6		
7			8		
9			10		
11			12		
13			14		
15			16		
17			18		
19			20		
21			22		
23			24		
25			26		
27			28		
29			30		
31					

B: MONTHLY RECORD OF HOME PRACTICE

Name _____

Month _____

DAY	MIN.	PARENT	DAY	MIN.	PARENT
1			2		
3			4		
5			6		
7			8		
9			10		
11			12		
13			14		
15			16		
17			18		
19			20		
21			22		
23			24		
25			26		
27			28		
29			30		
31					

B: MONTHLY RECORD OF HOME PRACTICE

Name _____

Month _____

DAY	MIN.	PARENT	DAY	MIN.	PARENT
1			2		
3			4		
5			6		
7			8		
9			10		
11			12		
13			14		
15			16		
17			18		
19			20		
21			22		
23			24		
25			26		
27			28		
29			30		
31					

C: SELECTED INSTRUMENT MANUFACTURERS

Orchestra Instruments

Glaesel Strings Div.
The Selmer Company
Box 310
Elkhart, IN 46515
(219) 522-1675

Knilling Strings Div.
St. Louis Music Co.
1400 Ferguson Ave.
St. Louis, MO 63133
(314) 727-4512

International Strings
NEMC
1181 Rt. 22, Box 1130
Mountainside, NJ 07092
(800) 526-4593

Yamaha Strings
Yamaha Corporation of America
PO Box 899
Grand Rapids, MI 49512
(616) 940-4900

Band Instruments

Blessing
1301 W. Beardsley
Elkhart, IN 46514
(800) 348-7409

Pearl International
PO Box 111240
Nashville, TN 37211
(615) 833-4477

Fox Products Corporation
6110 S SR5
South Whitley, IN 46787
(219) 723-4888

Ross Mallet Inst.
1304 First Ave.
Chippewa Falls, WI 54729
(715) 723-0807

Gemeinhardt
PO Box 788
Elkhart, IN 46515
(800) 348-7461

Selmer Corporation
Box 310
Elkhart, IN 46515
(219) 522-1675

Getzen
211 W. Centralia
Elkhorn, WI 53121
(414) 723-4221

United Musical Inst.
1000 Industrial Pkwy.
Elkhart, IN 46516
(800) 348-7610

Leblanc Corporation
7001 Leblanc Blvd.
Kenosha, WI 53141-1415
(800) 558-9421

Yamaha Corporation
PO Box 899
Grand Rapids, MI 49512
(616) 940-4900

D: OTHER MAIL ORDER SOURCES

Selected Mail-Order Music Dealers

Interstate Music Supply
13819 W. National Ave.
New Berlin, WI 53151
(414) 786-6210

NEMC
1181 Rt. 22, Box 1130
Mountainside, NJ 07092
(800) 526-4593

National Music Supply
PO Box 14421
St. Petersburg, FL 33733
(813) 823-6666

Woodwind & Brasswind
50731 U.S. 33 North
South Bend, IN 46637
(800) 348-5003

Music-Related Gifts

Friendship House
29313 Clemens Rd. #2-G
Cleveland, OH 44145-0623
(216) 871-8040

Music Treasures
327 Burnwick Rd.
Richmond, VA 23227
(804) 798-8613

Instrument Videos

Music Education Video
1108 Ridgecrest
Bowling Green, KY 42101
(502) 782-5258

E: SELECTED ASSOCIATIONS, MAGAZINES, INSURANCE

Associations

American Federation of Violin
& Bow Makers
2039 Locust St.
Philadelphia, PA 19103
(215) 567-4198

Music Distributors Association
135 W. 29th St.
New York, NY 10001
(212) 564-0251

NAPBIRT
PO Box 51
Normal, IL 61761
(309) 452-4257

National Music Council
10 Columbus Cir., 13th Fl.
New York, NY 10019

National School Music Dealers
PO Box 1209
513 Gillespie St.
Fayetteville, NC 28302
(919) 483-9032

Suzuki Assn. of the Americas
PO Box 354
Batterson Bldg.
Muscatine, IA 52761
(319) 263-3071

Music-Related Magazines

Instrumentalist
200 Northfield Rd.
Northfield, IL 60093
(312) 446-5000

Modern Drummer Magazine
870 Pompton Ave.
Cedar Grove, NJ 07009
(201) 239-4140

Music Magazine
Box 96, Station R
Toronto, Ontario M4G 3Z3
Canada

Strings Magazine
PO Box 767
San Anselmo, CA 94960

Instrument Insurance

American Bankers Ins. Co.
Music Agency, Inc.
PO Box 37285
Houston, TX 77237

Clarion Associates, Inc.
30 Lincoln Plaza, Suite 18-L
New York, NY 10023
(212) 541-7960

INDEX